ADVANCE PRAI

Skirting Here

"What a dazzling achievement. Elizabeth MacDonald vividly brings to life both the world of Medieval England and even more impressively, the heroic Margery Kempe, whose insights and courage speak to the modern world. This book will absorb and enlighten you."

—Steve Forbes, editor, *Forbes* Magazine

"One of the best historical narratives I've read in a long time. Elizabeth MacDonald has skillfully delivered a gripping, bold new take on a captivating historical figure, Margery Kempe, a story that shows what was happening in Catholic England before Joan of Arc was executed."

—Larry Kudlow, anchor, CNBC

"Elizabeth MacDonald is a gifted reporter—her ability to weave passion and truth together shines in *Skirting Heresy*. MacDonald's account of Margery Kempe's life is a compelling must-read story for religious readers and history buffs alike."

—Greta Van Susteren, host of *On the Record with Greta Van Susteren*

"Elizabeth MacDonald likely would hate being compared to a saint, but her writing here proves once again, her own inherent goodness. Few journalists reach such an understanding in life. Then again, few journalists come close to what my friend "Lizzy" has done in life, and the subjects she tackles routinely in life.... Quite a book. Quite a subject. Quite, an author."

—Neil Cavuto, host of *Cavuto* and *Your World with Neil Cavuto*

"Unable to read or write, Margery Kempe (1373–1438) is perhaps best known for dictating *The Book of Margery Kempe,* a work considered to be the first autobiography in the English language. Elizabeth MacDonald has written *Skirting Heresy: The Life and Times of Margery Kempe*...that were Ms. Kempe alive today, she, by necessity, could embrace the luxury of a recorded version of this wonderful account of her inspiring, quixotic life. Hallelujah!"

—Deirdre Imus, *New York Times* bestselling author

"Elizabeth MacDonald's story about Margery Kempe is an amazing historical perspective of a fascinating character that reads like a mystery you can't put down, full of passion and intrigue. I loved learning more about Margery—a strong medieval woman of faith taking a stand for what she believed in against all odds."
—Gretchen Carlson, host of *The Real Story with Gretchen Carlson*

"Elizabeth MacDonald has weaved together accounts from Margery's long-lost diary along with original and dogged reporting to present a narrative that is in itself a spiritual experience and mystery. The story unfolds as the mysteries of Kempe's life and extraordinary visions keep us riveted till the end. Finally, a critical figure in England's religious tumult leading to its rent from the Catholic Church is told and understood, shedding light on the modernization of Christendom. "
—David Asman, host of *Forbes on Fox*, cohost of *After the Bell*

"Elizabeth MacDonald has written a fresh, vivacious tale of extraordinary faith and courage, steeped in history but very modern. A must read!"
—Martha MacCallum, anchor, FOX News

"MacDonald has captured a remarkable story of courage and heroism. The values of Margery Kempe are timeless and need to be retold. Over and over again."
—Bill Hemmer, anchor, FOX News

"Margery Kempe's life story challenges all our notions of the path to sainthood. Was she a servant or a rebel? A Madonna or whore? Deeply devout or shrewdly heretical? Liz MacDonald tackles those many contradictions to bring Margery's character alive in haunting detail. You'll feel like you were in fifteenth-century England with the executioner lurking, and you'll be riveted from the get-go."
—Alisyn Camerota, anchor, FOX News

Skirting Heresy

. . .

THE
LIFE
AND
TIMES
OF
MARGERY
KEMPE

. . .

Elizabeth MacDonald

Franciscan
MEDIA
Cincinnati, Ohio

• • •

For my parents,
Regina and Hugh

• • •

Excerpts from Margery Kempe, *The Book of Margery Kempe*, B.A. Windeatt, trans., used by permission of Penguin Books, Ltd, 80 Strand, London WC2R 0RL. All rights reserved. Scripture passages have been taken from *New Revised Standard Version Bible*, copyright ©1989 by the Division of Christian Education of the National Council of the Churches of Christ in the U.S.A., and used by permission. All rights reserved.

Cover design by Kathleen Lynch | Black Kat Design
Cover image © Bridgeman Art Library
Book design by Mark Sullivan

LIBRARY OF CONGRESS CATALOGING-IN-PUBLICATION DATA
MacDonald, Elizabeth, 1962-
Skirting heresy : the life and times of Margery Kempe / by Elizabeth MacDonald.
pages cm
ISBN 978-1-61636-716-9 (alk. paper)
1. Kempe, Margery, approximately 1373- 2. Women mystics—England—Biography.
3. Mysticism—England—History—Middle Ages, 600-1500. I. Title.
BV5095.K4M33 2014
248.22092—dc23
[B]
2014002163
ISBN 978-1-61636-716-9

Published by Franciscan Media
28 W. Liberty St.
Cincinnati, OH 45202
www.FranciscanMedia.org

Printed in the United States of America.
Printed on acid-free paper.
14 15 16 17 18 5 4 3 2 1

CONTENTS

TIMELINE ... vii

PREFACE ... xi

CHAPTER ONE: *1417* ... 1

CHAPTER TWO: *1393* ... 11

CHAPTER THREE: *Evil Visitors* ... 14

CHAPTER FOUR: *Saved* ... 19

CHAPTER FIVE: *Bishop's Lynn* ... 25

CHAPTER SIX: *Turmoil* ... 32

CHAPTER SEVEN: *Neighbors Mock* ... 38

CHAPTER EIGHT: *1408* ... 47

CHAPTER NINE: *Marriage in Trouble* ... 50

CHAPTER TEN: *Backlash* ... 53

CHAPTER ELEVEN: *Priest Arrested* ... 57

CHAPTER TWELVE: *First Burned* ... 69

CHAPTER THIRTEEN: *Chastity in Marriage* ... 75

CHAPTER FOURTEEN: *Canterbury Monks* ... 82

CHAPTER FIFTEEN: *Patron Saint of Gossip* ... 87

CHAPTER SIXTEEN: *Arundel, then Julian* ... 94

CHAPTER SEVENTEEN: *Pilgrimage* ... 101

CHAPTER EIGHTEEN: *Battling Pilgrims* ... 108

CHAPTER NINETEEN: *Abandoned* ... 114

CHAPTER TWENTY: *Unexpected Reunion* ... 119

CHAPTER TWENTY-ONE: *The Holy Land* ... 124

CHAPTER TWENTY-TWO: *To Rome* ... 141

CHAPTER TWENTY-THREE: *Home to England* ... 149

CHAPTER TWENTY-FOUR: *Arrested* ... 158

CHAPTER TWENTY-FIVE: *Fighting for Her Life* ... 177

CHAPTER TWENTY-SIX: *Banished* ... 185

CHAPTER TWENTY-SEVEN: *Margery's Miracle* ... 193

CHAPTER TWENTY-EIGHT: *Passings* ... 200

BIBLIOGRAPHY ... 207

1348–1350	Great Plague in England
1353	First Statute of Praemunire
1366	King Henry IV born
1373	Margery Brunham born; St. Bridget of Sweden dies
1377	King Edward III dies; accession of King Richard II; Pope Gregory XI condemns John Wyclif's writings; first poll tax
1378	Papal schism
1379	Second poll tax
c1379	Wyclif's *De Eucharistia* rejects transubstantiation
1380–1381	Third poll tax; Peasants' Revolt
1382	Pope Gregory XI condemns Wyclif
1383	Henry le Despenser's failed Flemish crusade
1384	Wyclif dies
c1387–1390	General Prologue of Geoffrey Chaucer's *The Canterbury Tales*
1389–1390	*Opus Arduum*, attack on the church
c1390	Earliest version of Wycliffite Bible
1391–1393	Trial of Walter Brut, Lollard sympathizer
1393	Margery Brunham marries John Kempe; first child born; illness in childbirth; Great Statute of Praemunire
1393	Brewing and milling businesses fail
c1395	Twelve Conclusions of the Lollards
1397	Thomas Arundel's brother, Richard FitzAlan, beheaded

1399	Death of John of Gaunt, son of King Edward III, father of Henry Bolingbroke; Bolingbroke and Thomas Arundel banished; Bolingbroke crowned King Henry IV after deposing King Richard II; Arundel reinstated as Archbishop of Canterbury
1400	King Richard II dies; Geoffrey Chaucer dies; Owen Glendower uprising
1401	*De Haeretico Comburendo*, England's first death penalty for heresy; William Sawtrey, priest from Bishop's Lynn, burned as Lollard heretic
1403	Battle of Shrewsbury
1405	Northumberland revolt, Archbishop Richard Scrope executed
1408	Kempes embrace chastity in marriage
c1408–1409	Arundel's *Constitutions*; *The Lanterne of Light*, Lollard attack on the church
1410	John Badby burned as Lollard heretic; John Hus, Wyclif defender, excommunicated
c1410	Lollard Disendowment Bill presented to Parliament
1411	Margery says God ordered her to go on pilgrimage; Wyclif's books burned; Oxford University purge of Lollardy
1413	King Henry IV dies; accession of King Henry V; Lollard sympathizer Sir John Oldcastle escapes from Tower of London; Margery visits Bishop Philip Repingdon, Archbishop Arundel, Julian of Norwich; father John Brunham dies; Venice in winter
1414	Council of Constance to stop papal schism; Archbishop Arundel dies; Holy Land in spring; Rome in fall; Oldcastle's rebellion fails

1415	Home to England in spring; Henry V defeats French at Agincourt; John Hus, John Claydon, Richard Turming burned as heretics
1417	End of Great Schism; Kempe's pilgrimage to Santiago de Compostela; on trial for heresy in Leicester, York, Cawood, and Beverley in fall; Oldcastle executed
1418	Home in Bishop's Lynn, ill for eight months
1420	Famous Franciscan friar attacks Margery
1421	Great fire in Bishop's Lynn
1422	Death of King Henry V; accession of King Henry VI; Duke of Bedford named Regent of France
1423	William Taillour, priest, burned as Lollard heretic
1428–1431	Norwich heresy trials; William Chivelyng burned as Lollard heretic; priests William White, Fr. Abraham of Cholchester, John Waddon, William Caleys burned as heretics
1429	Joan of Arc's military successes for France
1431	Joan of Arc burned to death; William Perkins beheaded as Lollard heretic; Thomas Bagley burned as Lollard heretic; Margery's husband John and son die; King Henry VI crowned king of France
1433	Margery on pilgrimage to Aachen, Germany
1436	Margery starts dictating book
1438	Margery admitted to Bishop's Lynn's Guild of the Trinity
c1438–1440	Margery Kempe dies

I'd like to thank my agent, Karen Gantz Zahler, and my editors, Mary Carol Kendzia and Katie Carroll, Lindsay Roginski, and my friends and family, for their support in writing this book.

Skirting Heresy is neither an attempt to decode with perfect accuracy all of the facts that lay behind Margery Kempe's life, nor does it suggest all is known about Margery. This author is keenly aware that pinning down the historical Margery Kempe and imposing a chronological narrative on an unknown, complex world of facts can go too far. I surrender to readers who think what I've attempted questionable or objectionable.

This book is solely an attempt at a story, written with the fascination of an appreciative observer, of an unforgettable woman who lived in a difficult time in Catholic England. It was a time that crossed the deepest gullies and splits in history, a time that included the execution of Joan of Arc in 1431.

Margery's stream of consciousness memoir, *The Book of Margery Kempe*, was dictated to an anonymous scribe and written in Middle English around 1436. Though excerpts were being read aloud by the early part of the sixteenth century, soon Margery's memoir was abandoned. It went missing for five hundred years until its rediscovery in the private library of the Butler-Bowdon family in Lancashire in 1934 created a sensation.

Margery Kempe has since been admitted to the communion of Anglican saints. But along the way, she has also had a difficult time. She has been treated with contempt, caricatured, and dismissed as a self-promoting, hysterical neurasthenic, a vainglorious scold with God in her mind's eye always applauding her from behind.

That perception falls short, however, because Margery not only bravely reported all of her flaws, she gave us a story rich in detail, ringing with the quintessential, commonsense voices of medieval English people. I found myself connecting to a woman and a people from centuries ago who had the same anxieties and feelings we have today. People the world over can take great comfort in the gripping humanity and spirit of Margery's story.

Throughout my research, I felt the danger of filling in the blanks with perceptions and preoccupations. I tried to make the research as strong as possible, fleshing out details where none were to be found, hoping they were plausible and made sense. After all, I owe Margery the care and research she deserves, although I was always aware I would fall short. I've especially tried to understand her husband John, who appears in her memoirs as a half-written character, only in outline, a conundrum. The children don't appear at all.

Worth noting here is an exercise I did with Margery's memoirs. I tend to read newspaper stories backwards, because journalists often top load stories and bury the best information in the remaining paragraphs. I did the same with Margery's memoir, and in doing so, I saw something besides, say, Margery's quotations from the works of mystics like Richard Rolle or St. Bridget. Instead, I repeatedly saw a motion for the defense. And in understanding and seeing beyond that, I was struck by how other voices kept coming out, hilarious and colorful ones at that: "Why do you weep so much, Margery? Jesus is long since dead." "His mother never wept as much for him." "Your tears are angel's drink."

Most of all, the exercise revealed the story of a human being who courageously engaged in electrifying, gladiatorial battles with the most powerful men of the Catholic Church, clashes that turned carnivalesque while bureaucrats fumed and the stake loomed for the insufferable. Margery's story is the stuff of true adventure.

No one will ever know if Margery really did have visions of Jesus and the saints. But as Julian of Norwich tells us, we operate with a limited set of five senses that cannot know the ultimate reality. Noteworthy here is that arctic reindeer can see ultraviolet light and certain birds can see colors humans cannot. I've always been appreciative of what the physicist Richard Smalley, who theorized about atomic particles, once said: "How can we know what we cannot see?" In other words, isn't it easy to know everything when one knows nothing?

Religious faith is often not about historical context, but about the possibility of the human spirit. The dangerous, unpopular, and uncomfortable vocation of holy tears coursing down Margery's face takes the Christian witness out of airless, hyper-abstract, denatured debates and right back to where the Christian faith began—at the cross. It's at the intersections where life begins, the cross the ultimate one.

Margery's story is about a faith that shows humankind another way: the pilgrim's road. It is a story of that faith I hoped to tell. I thank you for reading it.

CHAPTER ONE

1417

*S*eptember turned out to be an unusually cold month to be thrown out of yet another northern town. Twilight had already begun to fall by four o'clock, the afternoon was turning bitterly cold.

Two solitary figures were making their way with great difficulty along a road tracked with deep, icy ruts stiff as wood heading south out of York in northern England. Bare trees stood exposed under a deepening autumn sky, the cold wind not lifting the travelers' spirits. There were no welcoming crowds, no chiming church bells, no friends. Only frozen road.

For as long as she lived, Margery Kempe would never forget this time, for the die was finally cast. She would either live or be put to death in a vicious burning at the stake. Now her fate depended on one thing: her own tongue.

Her appointed escort, John, the Archbishop of York's man, was under strict orders to get Margery out of town after she was just barely found innocent of heresy at trial. The two finally made it to Hessle on the banks of the river Humber, more than thirty-five miles away from York. The plan was for Margery to take a ferryboat across the river and then hurry home to Bishop's Lynn.

But two friars had secretly followed Margery out of York. They had attended all of her trials and hearings, had fumed at her outrageous attacks on the clergy, and had taken note how she repeatedly dodged the stake. They were enraged that Margery had once again duped a church leader into letting her escape.

To her many detractors, Margery was not just a woman who clearly enjoyed sex to the point of having fourteen children, now dressed in white pretending to be a virgin nun, arrogantly lecturing about the Gospels when even freelance preaching about the Bible was against the law.

They saw Margery as the leading female figure of a subversive heretic movement sweeping the country, yet another distracting revolt from within when barbaric invaders from Scotland and Wales were on England's doorstep. The country was at a violent tipping point yet again. Danger was out on the streets, a certain moral panic gripped the population, now rife with suspicion and revenge.

The friars went straight to the top, to the second-most powerful man in England, to put an end to Margery for good. They tracked down two guardsmen of the formidable, beak-nosed brother of King Henry V, John of Lancaster, keeper of the realm while the king was away at war in France pursuing claims to the French throne. Henry V had appointed Lancaster the Duke of Bedford. He was so powerful that Lancaster would later be named commander-in-chief of France as well.

The duke's men were in the area helping to lead a punishing reprisal attack on invading Scots joined with Lollard heretics. Yet his men were celebrating. They had finally captured the leader of the Lollard underground, the cantankerous outlaw knight, John Oldcastle. The court would soon burn him alive in the most horrific way yet invented—hung by chains lashed around his middle and slow-roasted over a fire, then disemboweled and dismembered, the duke looking on.

The friars raced on horseback into Beverley, a town thirty miles east of York, and found the duke's yeomen. They were supposed to be on patrol but were instead drinking in a local tavern. The friars quickly relayed Margery's crimes.

"Margery Kempe is one of the most evil deceivers who ever lived," one said to the guards, who ignored him as they ate.

Seeing he was not making any headway, the other said more forcefully, "This daughter of a former member of Parliament is the consort of that black spirit, Oldcastle. She has said enough to burn twenty heretics."

The yeomen had heard enough. They had caught wind that a female might be leading the Lollard underground, but they had never heard her name. A daughter of such high social status made perfect sense. They pulled back on their coats and re-strapped their leather bracers to their arms. They then grabbed their bows, arrows, and swords, and raced away on their horses, picking up information as to Margery's whereabouts along the way.

Just as she was about to step on board a rowboat to cross the river Humber in Hessle, one of the yeomen threw himself from his mount and marched up to Margery. "Our lord, the Duke of Bedford, has sent for you," he yelled, as Margery looked up, startled.

The other growled, "You are held to be the greatest Lollard in all this part of the country, or around London. We have sought you in many a part of the land." With that, they locked her wrists in metal cuffs. Margery went white. Always chaffering for cash, they agreed arresting Margery would be a quick way to make money. "We shall have a hundred pounds for bringing you before our lord," one gloated.

Triumphant, the yeomen led Margery toward their horses, as she said, her head bowed, "With a good will, sirs, I shall go with you wherever you will lead me."

Margery had finally done it. She had landed in the upper reaches of the court and was about to be caught in its grinding, calculating machine, where justice was unemotionally doled out, unswayed by gender. Margery had angered the country's most dangerous men, the same merciless group led by the Duke of Bedford who would later usher Joan of Arc to the stake.

Through a dim countryside the party trotted at a clipped pace, a sad, dispirited procession, heading back toward Beverley. Margery rode pillion in chains on a jennet pony behind. A fat yellow sun eased down toward the horizon, a faint quarter moon slowly mounting. Off in the distance, a remote breeze from an ancient grotto hidden deep in the woods tossed twigs off the birch trees up ahead, the yeomen ducking their heads under sharp edges as men in houses and taverns beyond began lighting fires in their hearths. After riding for some time in the numbing cold, the group arrived at an inn a mile or so outside Beverley where they would stay the night.

The next morning as they rode through the outskirts of town, Margery sat up against the high pommel of her saddle, startled to see her reputation had preceded her. Women clamored out of the front doors of their houses waving their distaffs used to spin wool, shouting at them, "Burn this false heretic."

Farmers working in the fields on the side of the road grew upset at the sight of Margery in chains. "Woman, give up this life that you lead and go and spin, and card wool, as other women do," they yelled. "We would not suffer so much for any money on earth."

Margery said loudly, "I do not suffer as much sorrow as I would do for our Lord's love, for I only suffer cutting words. It is truly nothing that I suffer, in comparison to what he suffered."

Meanwhile, one of the friars whispered to the yeomen, "Let her prattle on, she'll fashion a noose of words to hang herself with."

But one of the guards grew uneasy, because along the way, Margery gave them advice on how to be better Christians. Perhaps she really was a saint. He finally said as they stopped to rest, "I rather regret that I met with you, for it seems to me that you speak very good words."

A flush of gratitude brightened her face as Margery replied, "Sir, do not regret nor repent that you met with me. Do your lord's will, and I trust that all shall be for the best, for I am very well pleased that you met with me." That made him more nervous, so instead of taking her to jail, he locked Margery in a room at an inn. John, her escort, was temporarily imprisoned but released the next day, stalking away in anger.

A crowd grew outside Margery's window, some incensed about this accused Lollard heretic. Others were merely curiosity seekers, for this was the town of Beverley, home to its own famous female fighter who had battled with crusaders against Saladin, the sultan of Egypt, in the siege of Jerusalem in 1187.

"Didn't our Margaret just like this woman, Margery, go on pilgrimage to Jerusalem?" a miller asked a baker, who ignored him. He said more stridently as people continued to arrive, "Yes, our pilgrim Margaret wearing only a cook pot on her head as a helmet, brave as Judith who slew the tyrant Holofernes. But didn't our Margaret escape from the Saracens?"

Soon, Margery spotted an opportunity. Her second-floor window-sill was the perfect pulpit. Now she could talk freely in her enemies' absence, since the duke's men had gone off to town to announce her capture. Margery entertained the crowd with colorful stories of Jerusalem, Rome, and Compostela. They listened, riveted, since most had not ventured beyond the city gates. Soon a chorus yelled up at her, "Alas, woman, why should you be burned?"

Margery, though, shushed them with a wave of her hand. "I am thirsty. I yearn for a drink," she called rather theatrically to the yeoman's wife through the door.

"Didn't Jesus say these same words on Mt. Calvary?" one woman asked another, and they started to sob. Meanwhile, the wife of the inn's owner yelled churlishly back, "My husband has the key to your room. I can't get you anything."

Hearing that, the crowd took offense. "They have locked up a holy woman with nothing to drink," a young girl protested. They ran to a barn, grabbed a ladder, and quickly raised it up to Margery's second-floor window. The girl scrambled up with a pint of wine in a pot and a cup. "Quick, hide this under your bed so the guards won't see it," she warned.

The miller again asked, "But our Margaret escaped, why doesn't Margery just escape down the ladder?" As Margery drank, a growing number in the crowd yelled up at her, "Escape." But she felt an overwhelming need to stay. Something was coming. Margery then bowed her head, knelt, and began to pray, only the top of her strawberry-blonde head showing at the windowsill, as the crowd slowly dispersed in the gathering darkness.

Nighttime approached. The medieval world of men and their crude machines fell silent. But Margery was wide awake; she couldn't sleep. It was very dark outside. Suddenly, a loud voice boomed, "Margery."

She sat bolt upright, then shut her eyes tight and prayed as fast and as hard as she could, because this vision scared her. It was too real. Jesus said, "Daughter, it is more pleasing to me that you suffer scorn and humiliation, shame and rebukes, wrongs and distress than if your head were struck off three times a day every day for seven years."

This vision was intense and confusing. Margery couldn't tell if it meant she was going to live or die. Tears came to her eyes, and she shivered. Jesus continued, "You have great cause to rejoice, for when you come home to heaven, then shall every sorrow be turned into joy for you."

That message was ominous. The end was near. Margery drifted off into a fitful, dreamless sleep. Dawn crept grey and dreary across her window. She rubbed her eyes, rolled out of bed, and began to put on her white mantle. Outside there was a bustle of men, commotion, and then guards banged on her door. "Come with us now," they ordered.

They again slapped metal handcuffs on her wrists and marched Margery over to the chapter house of St. John's Church in Beverley. A tribunal of the most powerful men of the church would now decide whether to advise the Duke of Bedford that Margery should be put to death.

There stood the sublimely irritable Henry Bowet, Archbishop of York, surrounded by senior clerics glaring at Margery. Archbishop Bowet was a personal friend to kings, but he was growing old. He was about to be carried on a litter back into battle to boost the morale of the English army in the north as they tried to beat back the invading Scots.

Now he was exasperated, not looking forward to yet another trial of this nuisance. "What, woman, have you come back again? I would gladly be rid of you," Archbishop Bowet fumed, as he walked toward his chair and she looked down at the ground.

As the clerics joined him at the front of the hearing room, the archbishop ordered Margery, "Take yourself out into the middle of the court and address us from there."

A priest took Margery by the hand as she delicately walked to the middle of the room. The crowd leaned forward as Archbishop Bowet swiftly turned to her judges and said, "Sirs, I had this woman before me at Cawood and there I with my clerics examined her in her faith and found no fault in her."

The women in the crowd from the night before murmured, "Weren't these the same words Pontius Pilate said in front of Jesus?" They again started to cry.

The archbishop saw and spoke louder, "Furthermore, sirs, I have since that time spoken with good men who hold her to be a perfect woman and a good woman."

The archbishop reminded the gathering over the loud chattering, "I gave one of my men five shillings to lead her out of this part of the country, in order to quieten the people down. And as they were going on their journey they were taken and arrested, my man put in prison because of her."

A monk who detested Margery scoffed, "Money clearly wasted."

Glaring at him, the archbishop recounted, "Her gold and her silver was taken away from her, together with her beads and her ring, and she is brought here before me again. Is there any man here who can now say anything against her?"

The women in the crowd said in unison, "She's a good woman."

But a dark-haired Dominican friar elbowed his way to the front of the crowd. "Here is a friar who knows many things against her," the monk crowed.

The friar stood right behind Margery, smoothed his robes, and declared, "Margery Kempe has mocked the men of holy church for years. She preaches the Gospel, just like a heretic Lollard, and that is against the law. She is a fraud. Her hysterical weeping for Jesus and talk of visions are done for show."

When Margery turned around, her jaw dropped open. It was her lifelong enemy who had stalked her for most of her adult life and studiously collected proof of her every error. But before she could react, the friar then loudly declared the thing that always shocked Margery to the pith of her being and caused her to visibly buckle at the knees.

"Margery Kempe should have been burnt at Bishop's Lynn had my good fellows of the friar preachers there not intervened to stop it," he announced, as the crowd surged forward, stomping their feet, whistling and catcalling.

Shouting over the tumult, the friar larded on his proof, "And sir, she says that she may weep and have contrition when she will. Because God somehow talks to her in visions, so no need for a priest in confession. But that, as we all know, is heresy."

Then came the final blow. The two guardsmen who had arrested Margery stepped forward and stood next to the friar to deliver the fatal charge, "Most importantly, Margery Kempe is the consort of Sir John Oldcastle. Margery Kempe is his messenger, delivering Oldcastle's orders of heresy, anarchy, and sedition to the enemies of the crown around the country."

As the crowd roared disapproval, one of the guardsmen yelled over the ruckus, "Everywhere she goes, Margery Kempe incites rebellion, she agitates and upsets the people."

Another monk in the crowd shouted helpfully into the tumult, "Or maybe Margery is just a wandering nun?"

The yeomen were pushed further forward and one cried, "Tell us, too, has anyone ever proved that she really went on pilgrimage to Jerusalem or Rome?" Now the age-old, ugly rumor resurfaced once again to usher Margery along to the stake.

The Dominican friar who disliked Margery stepped forward, pointed an accusing finger at her, and said emphatically to the tribunal, "Margery Kempe is an adulterous liar. She has never gone to the Holy Land or Rome. She instead went into hiding because she got pregnant from sleeping with men on her travels."

Chaos ensued. Chairs and stools were overturned, as gossips loudly clucked, "So that's the truth, pilgrimages as a pretense to run off into the woods to enjoy the lust of her body."

The monk scoffed at Margery, "Pilgrimage to sinful couplings, is that what your new religion preaches, Margery? Is that how you came about your whelping fourteen times over, you lewd callet?"

The Dominican friar then turned around to Margery and hissed, "We've got you now. You're finished. Your vainglory will soon end in a heap of cinders."

The crowd banged on tables, roaring support either for or against Margery. Humiliated, she remained silent, staring at the ground, bitter tears biting the sides of her eyes and running down her nose.

Archbishop Bowet thundered, "Enough." The entire hearing room fell silent, unsettled. "Speak, Margery, what do you have to say in your defense?" he demanded.

The crowd turned toward her. The climactic moment was here. Now, only a thin fence as fine as a thread stood between Margery and a burning at the stake. Her soul writhed in sheer terror.

CHAPTER TWO

1393

*M*argery sat up gasping from throbbing pain. Her white linen tunic was yanked high above her hips, her head bent forward. Her bed sheet was wet and twisted.

A cold arctic breeze streamed over her windowsill from the North Sea. An early November snow blanketed the countryside from river to seacoast outside her bedroom window. The sand at the seashore was gritty on the surface but packed solid four feet down from the severe cold, snowdrifts banked against fieldstone walls. Blasts of sea wind bent evergreen trees down toward the ground. Resigned, accustomed to winter, the branches bowed toward Margery's window, just as she was resigned to laboring mightily.

Class and status didn't matter now, much as it mattered to her. She was just like any other woman in childbirth, not talking, for once. Margery was giving birth to her first baby and the grandson of a popular mayor of Bishop's Lynn, a veteran of Parliament.

Margery and her family were prominent in this seacoast town in England of about 5,500, nearly a hundred miles northeast of London. Perched on the Great Ouse River, Bishop's Lynn delivered vital goods to the countryside, as well as income and loans to King Richard II's bankrupt treasury. The kings of England and nobles of the royal court visited frequently.

But Margery's high social status would soon be upended for good, not because she was about to be a new mother. Margery would swear, and her confessors would concur, that Jesus, his Blessed Mother Mary, Mary's mother St. Anne, Mary Magdalene, Saints Peter, Paul, Jerome, Margaret of Antioch, and Catherine of Alexandria spoke to her, as did Lucifer.

For her visions, her lecturing, her public sobbing, and much more, Margery Kempe was about to become one of the most talked about women in medieval England. Moreover, this woman who couldn't read or write would become the first known autobiographer in the English language. Yet on this simple winter's day, Margery was merely trying to give birth to a baby boy. "Push," a stout, freckled midwife ordered.

Frustrated, Margery tried again, her long, strawberry-blonde hair plumed out around her ears and pasted to her high, perspiring forehead. An icy breeze cooled the pink glow of her round face, the chin receding slightly, her nose long and sharp.

But just as Margery pushed up on her elbows, her sturdy twenty-year-old body suddenly buckled and collapsed. Her blue eyes were lit with fear. Something was terribly wrong. A deadly bacterial infection was trying to claim her life and the life of her newborn baby boy.

As her body grew prickly hot, Margery panicked. Crying, arms flailing, she struggled to break free of a nursemaid trying to stuff a rag in her mouth. Meanwhile, a dairymaid turned midwife gently massaged Margery's womb with oils as another helped her struggling newborn son out into the twilight years of the fourteenth century. A wet nurse busily handed over linen bandages, a knife to cut the umbilical cord, and salt to rub on the baby to ward off the devil.

As he heard the women clamoring about overhead, shouting, "More water. She's dropping," Margery's husband, John Kempe, remained downstairs, worried, helpless, as custom banned him from the birthing chamber. John stared up at the ceiling, then out the kitchen window at a church spire jabbing the sky in the middle distance. Peals of thunder sounded a warning as a winter squall slapped gusts of icy rain against the window glass. He watched, distracted, as a huddle of sheep hurried past to seek shelter from the storm.

John should be thrilled now, but he, too, was in pain. A mystery was upon him. His wife was keeping a dark secret from him. Despite attempts by disapproving priests to stop it, Margery attracted men. She was ambitious, constantly straining against roles imposed on medieval women, that of wife, mother, or nun. Margery was also vain, increasingly irritable, and moody, "stubborn as a bull's foot," in the words of a local friar.

Hours later, Margery awakened, her birth canal wadded with linen to stop the bleeding. Her newborn son slept peacefully in a nursemaid's arms. John noticed that as she kissed their baby on his forehead, his wife then looked away, distracted. What John couldn't know was that Margery grew steadily horrified over a mysterious sin of the flesh that could bring about not only her destruction, but also the ruination of their family's sterling name. It was a secret sin she could tell no one about, not even her devoted husband. As John looked on wondering, Margery wept uncontrollably, certain she was doomed to an eternity in hell.

CHAPTER THREE

Evil Visitors

*M*argery tried to heal, but she was inconsolable. She couldn't shake this shame and privately grieved her sin into an inky blackness unmoored from reality. Like a massive bruise under her robe, her feelings of guilt caused her to flinch at her husband's embrace. Margery felt lost, exhausted, her unrelenting melancholy pinched down hard on her head like a tight prelate's skullcap. Her illness reawakened fears that suddenly dying without confession meant eternal damnation.

As soon as she could, Margery arranged for her confessor, Fr. Robert Spryngolde, to come to her home to hear her confession, still too sick to go to church on her own. Fr. Spryngolde had known Margery and her family for years, which made her sin of the flesh feel even more shameful. She was convinced nothing could lift this anchor off her soul. Her feelings were made worse by a Lollard in town who had convinced Margery that she didn't need to go to confession, that she could do penance all by herself.

As Fr. Spryngolde sat in a chair beside her bed, Margery got up and knelt by his side, made the sign of the cross, and in a tiny, thimble voice began, "Benedicite," to which he replied, "Dominus." After she talked a little while, Margery ventured, "Father, I also have a heart of vanity that caused me to…" But she lost her nerve and wavered.

Fr. Robert had already seen her confession in her eyes. Instead of giving her comfort, he suddenly shocked Margery by cutting her off. "Do not speak if you cannot say this sin," he scolded. "The mouth is the gateway to heaven or hell."

Margery gasped as if a herring bone was stuck in her throat. After an awkward silence, she stuttered, "Thank you, Father." He stood up, blessed her with the sign of the cross, and left.

Outside her bedroom window, the light from a three o'clock sun struck the countryside off kilter. As yellow, red, and orange leaves fell slanted in droves, Margery's mind was swirling. Her deepest fear had come to pass. Damnation loomed. "Die I will, unforgiven, because I do not deserve to be forgiven," she said to the trees outside.

Later, alone and worn out, Margery waited in the darkness of her bedroom for John. Her baby boy had finally fallen asleep in his narrow truckle bed across the bedroom after fussing under a grey wool blanket. John had gone to town, but had taken a brief detour back home, walking through the woods, confused. He was not interested in the entertainment that other men enjoyed, the bull or bear baiting. As the afternoon world grew hushed, John laid down under a tree and drifted off to sleep. Back home, Margery fell asleep too, her nursemaids dozing, wrapped in blankets by the fire.

Suddenly, Margery's bedroom hurtled into a cindery black tunnel. What had terrorized her all her life was now happening. Demonic visitations. Margery's bedroom beyond the foot of her bed sucked violently inward into a monstrous vacuum and curved into a hole in the upper left. Suddenly, she saw the hole burst open and demons come barreling forth. They rushed Margery's bed and crowded at her shoulders, lunging at her neck.

Margery tried to escape to the right side of her bed, but a lower demon was already squatted on the floor at her head. In a thin, reedy voice he mocked in her face, "Margereee, why did you ever think your Jesus King would forgive you?" An echo chamber of malevolent laughter burst open behind him from demons who were human souls unshriven, disfigured by sin. Suddenly, it all stopped.

Quivering and sweating, Margery looked around. The room was coal black as night. "No, no, no," she cried out, frozen solid in panic. "John, where are you?" Her nursemaids woke up and looked at each other, puzzled.

Then suddenly a ferocious wind lifted the demons up off the ground and tossed them against her bedroom wall. Just as rapidly, the room collapsed into a black pinpoint at the foot of her bed, into a place where life could not survive.

As Margery strained to see, the pinpoint blew open into a yawning wind tunnel. As the belly of gravity dropped out of the room, Margery was pinned on her straw mattress. A fat nursemaid had rushed into the room and had lain across Margery's chest to hold her arms down. Eyes rigid with horror, Margery could only move her head as her nursemaids tried desperately to console her back in the world. "What is that? Who is there?" Margery shouted, paralyzed with fear.

Then out of the darkness he came. Satan walked to the foot of Margery's bed and stood staring at the ground, the outline of his body indistinct, grainy. Margery was now in the fight of her life. She wrenched her body from side to side, as her maids pushed her back down and frantically mopped her forehead.

Then suddenly, right behind Satan, the fireplace beyond the foot of her bed blew open into a panoramic vista of hell. Margery was yanked upward above the gaping jaws of a furnace below her feet. The nurses looked at each other, surprised that some curious strength was overtaking Margery.

From below her feet in her vision, leathery devils with flames pouring out of their mouths, ears, and nostrils jumped up at her, angrily clutching at her ankles. They flew up like black moths and tried to swallow her head. She was aghast to see their stomachs were lit with raging fires. Margery punched, clawed, and kicked at her nursemaids, but they finally pushed her back down on her mattress. Then it got worse.

Because Margery had broken one of the Ten Commandments, now Satan came forward with his own. He had been standing at the foot of her bed, but a split-second later he was two inches from Margery's face, staring deep into her soul, no eyes, just dark holes.

"Reject God, Jesus, his Mother, the apostles, and all the saints," Satan commanded. "Reject your Christian faith, good works, all virtues, your family, and your friends."

Terrified, Margery screamed, "I reject God, Jesus, the Blessed Mother, my family, my friends, and the entire heavenly host."

Satan ordered, "You desire only me and me alone."

Margery yelled, "I desire only wickedness."

He grinned, "Wicked is your family."

Margery replied, distraught, "Wicked are my family and friends. I am evil."

Meanwhile, John had met his friend William out on the road, and the two were just now walking in the front door downstairs. Hearing Margery, they stared at each other in shock. Then the worst happened.

"Kill yourself," Satan commanded.

Anguished, Margery tried to commit suicide. She viciously bit the only part of her body that was free, her hand, blood pouring out, a vivid red scar that could be seen for the rest of her life. A nursemaid ran downstairs. "Margery is trying to kill herself," she cried out to John.

Panicked, John and William raced upstairs and into the bedroom. They tried to hold Margery down, but she kicked at them, got free, and escaped toward the stairs, in danger of falling headlong to the first floor.

Hearing the commotion, neighbors came running, their friends Catherine, her husband Thomas, and William's wife Eleanor. They clamored upstairs and finally tied Margery down to her bed. But that didn't work, because Margery ripped her hands free and bit at her hands, still trying to kill herself. She tore at her heart with her nails, scratching to gouge out the secret, evil sin.

"It is the fever. It's just the fever," her nursemaids pleaded with John.

"But if she kills herself, Margery will be damned for all eternity," Eleanor warned.

John asked, "Should I call for the priest to bring absolution?"

Not knowing how else to save her, they carried Margery into a storage room, and used the ropes and chains on a trunk to tie her down for her own good. They quickly set up a small bed for her to rest on. Margery would remain in that storage room for eight long months, sick in mind and body, misunderstood, still trying any chance she could to kill herself. The traumatic visions continued, of malevolent demons who took pleasure in assaulting her night and day. No one, not even John, could rescue Margery now.

CHAPTER FOUR

Saved

*M*onths passed. To try and bring his wife back to reality, John cooked comfort foods for Margery. He fed her three times a day with warm caudles, meat stew with peas and dark rye bread, or oatmeal puddings with whinberries and spiced cream. John gently bathed her and also tended to their new baby boy.

Catherine and Eleanor visited often, daily bathing the baby, combing Margery's hair, doing laundry, scrubbing the house clean to ward off infant mortality, which was notoriously high in the area due to all manner of diseases, plague, tuberculosis, the bloody flux, and small pox.

Catherine regularly pulled down bundles of straw someone kept trying to hang above the Kempes' front door to signal infection within. William left a bucket of fresh milk on the stoop each morning, sometimes carrying two in his shovel hands with the squared-off nails. But all Margery could do was blankly stare back at her friends, then turn away. "She may not live," Doctor Gunther warned John.

One morning eight months later, Margery slept quietly on her bed. Long ago the ropes and chains tying her down had been removed, though she was still very sick. Later that morning, John went out to meet Catherine, who wanted to see once and for all whether the doctor was incompetent. They walked over to his shop downtown, a painted wooden sign of a single bandaged arm hanging over his door.

Doctor Gunther cut hair, did surgeries, set broken bones, and pulled teeth. He came to the Kempes' house once every other week to check Margery's humors—choler, phlegm, black bile, and blood. Today, John had dutifully delivered Margery's urine in a wooden cup. "How goes her water?" he asked, anxious, as the doctor eyeballed the color and consistency. "Same," the doctor said as John looked down at the floor. Catherine, though, was fed up.

"After eight months, the same response, 'same.' Is that the best you can do?" she demanded. Catherine followed him as the doctor went outside. "Why do you think I have this sign above my shop, because I sell arms for a living?" he shot back.

But Catherine drew herself up and coolly replied, "I will not pretend it was my idea to hire you to take care of my friend. The last time I spoke with you, you said the bump on my back meant I had five months to live. The fact that I've outlived that judgment six years now, the fact that all you can still say after eight months now is 'same,' will never increase my diminishing trust in you."

The doctor harrumphed, "Your opinion."

"Yes, but you make money off yours," she retorted, her parting shot bouncing off his back as he marched away.

Back at home, Margery's nursemaids had gone to town. The lower devils were still squatting in the corner of her bedroom, keeping watch. Suddenly, they looked up, stunned, and vanished. All fell eerily silent.

Margery heard a noise and, exhausted, sat up in bed, fearful. The fire on her cheeks had strangely cooled into a mist. Margery patted her face. Suddenly, with great force and clarity the day turned brilliant. As she looked up, her mouth fell wide open, her eyes big as pewter dish plates. Margery had an astounding vision.

Jesus walked in, wrapped in a purple silk robe, radiating a love that she had never felt before. Margery watched Jesus as he gently sat on her bed, turned a face of kindness toward her, and asked, "Daughter, why have you rejected me when I have never, not even for one minute, rejected you?"

Then just as suddenly, a shaft of light broke into the room, and without waiting for her answer, Margery watched Jesus rise up, slowly, so that she could behold him until he disappeared.

Finally, after all this time, Margery was forgiven. Her world was new again. Jesus loved her no matter what, despite all her petty jealousies, vanities, and judgments. Yet there was something more. She had seen something beyond the boundary of all that was reasonable. After all these years searching, she had found the true love of her life, but he wasn't of the earth.

So now Margery would love Jesus for the rest of her life with a growing passion that would upend her family for good. She would soon spend the rest of her days impatiently searching for him, tirelessly crisscrossing the world at a time of mounting danger, when women were largely housebound and the average Englishman journeyed no farther than two miles from his place of birth. And even though her husband had fought so hard to beat back every rival to win Margery, he was about to lose her for good.

John entered the storage room with her breakfast of eggs, hard bacon, and dark bread. He quickly saw his wife's eyes were bright again, the color back in her cheeks. Margery said simply, "I am hungry."

Soon their friends, their household help, all came piling in to hug her. All were as strangers before. But no longer. Margery ate ravenously, like a starving girl, looking up at John and their friends, content, wrapped in the laziness of a warm blanket. When Margery finished eating, she still wanted more. She asked, "May I have the keys to the pantry to take my meat and drink on my own?"

But distrustful of her new demeanor, Margery's maidservants pulled John aside and warned, "Do not give her the keys. She'll just give away everything you own, all of your ale, wine, your food. She's still not of her right mind."

John ignored them. "Give her the keys."

John loved Margery for a whole range of reasons, for her compassion, her identification with others, her toothy, ironic smile. His young wife was a rarity. She was confident, gifted with a certain charisma, a sharp mind, and abundant generosity.

But Margery was also a puzzle. Strong-willed and uncompromising, she radiated passion, a duality of ocean liner strength and vulnerable sensitivity. "Margery is vain. Many men stare at her," his friends William and Thomas had tried to warn John years before, but he hardly heard a word.

Margery's interior weather was electric, while John's was placid, almost compulsively solitary. Though he put on a pleasant face, he was given to bouts of extreme loneliness. He liked the comfortable, livable status quo of silence. At home, they shared a frankness and love of sex, though Margery was increasingly distracted. As their family grew in size, she became even more of a riddle.

At Mass in St. Margaret's cathedral, a towering church of sugary limestone, Margery would sit bolt upright, transfixed by the crucifix, Jesus's body arched painfully outward on the cross. She avidly listened to sermons, but she was unable to read or write. Like most of the population, she was scarcely literate.

But while Margery sat infatuated with the radiance of Mass, John sat smitten with his children, watching his babies running around trying to pull out the lit white tallow candles stuck on the wooden rails at the side chapels. Their dimpled faces beamed at him from under their caps when they climbed up his shoulders.

Back home, John would sometimes ask, uncertain feelings producing an uncertain smile, "Maybe you and I can take a walk to the shore?" The quiet susurration of the ocean waves were appealing. But Margery wouldn't answer, lost in prayer.

John was not good with money, and neither was Margery. She fell prey to vanity, reveling in how men and women admired how she looked, jealous if they were dressed as well as she. Margery loved buying bright colored clothes in flamboyant styles just in from the continent, fine cloaks of rich scarlet or purple with dagged edges slashed with emerald or cornflower yellow, trimmed with marten fur.

Worried, John watched his wife twirl about barefoot through the rushes and bay leaves on the floor of their whitewashed stone house. An odd new thing was on her head. It was a fashionable crespine, a gaudy hat shaped into two gold horns fitted with mesh that only the wealthy wore in the social swirl of the upper classes in Bishop's Lynn.

"I shall be all the more stared at and worshiped," Margery gloated as she took off the crespine.

"She'll have to walk sideways into church with that monstrosity on her head," her neighbor Ruth had sniped in the shop in town where Margery had bought it.

Meanwhile, John was asking, "Our family is growing in size, why spend our money on frivolous things? Isn't it better to leave such vanity behind?"

What did her husband know of fashion, son of a low-born leather merchant? Margery whirled on him, "I come from noble kindred and will wear clothes that uphold the honor of my family. Perhaps you should never have married me."

That hurt John. For a little while longer, they worked quietly in the kitchen. But Margery couldn't take his silence nor her guilt. So she did what she always did when her mind got too jumpy. She walked alone down to the shore of the North Sea, pensive, detaching the wimple draped below her chin from ear to ear that held the faces of medieval women like chalices. It wasn't the quiet murmur of the ocean Margery wanted. It was the thunder of crashing waves to blot out her conflicting feelings.

"Even when we think he is far away, Jesus is always near with his mercy and grace," Margery said aloud as she walked.

. . .

Bishop's Lynn

Although the wintry scene at the shore was stunningly bleak, Margery loved the desolate landscape. To her it was beautiful. Past sedge and bulrush, past salt marsh and sand dunes she walked, mill wheels gently turning in rivers in the distance. She stood looking out over the distant shoreline, wet, cold sand clasping her ankles like a soothing poultice, amid the samphire and comb jellyfish. Margery watched a wave cresting a little off shore, the white foam furling as it glided forward and finally crashed down, spanning out before her toes.

There was no escaping water in Bishop's Lynn. Its every rolling hillside or sloping byway eventually led to the North Sea, the Ouse River, or the Great Wash. The sea was full of life, full of fish, full of oysters, full of longing, of seagulls wheeling, placid calm and storms, never sated, its waves a constant companion.

Because they were hemmed in by water all around, the people of Bishop's Lynn lived in daily fear of flooding or drowning, dead sailors discovered on shore like something out of an anxiety dream. The town sat perched between the Great Ouse River and the sea, transected by the Purfleet, or tidal channel, to the north and the Millfleet to the south. Town officials, like Margery's father John Brunham, at great expense ordered numerous sluices, canals, and walls built against storm surges as the sea fought to reclaim the land, the littoral Lynn stood on easily overwhelmed by water. Locals talked anxiously about hurricanes of years past, like the great hurricane that hit nearby Dunwich in East Anglia in 1347, sweeping the entire town out into the ocean in the dead of night, two churches and about four hundred houses, men, women, and children still in their beds.

The heart of the town was built around St. Margaret's Church, which sat between the two fleets, with town offices, guildhalls, shops, and warehouses standing near a compact, gossipy warren of houses on narrow streets.

Margery's husband John and their friends ran to and fro in Lynn's beaver community of merchants, working in the booming sea trade of the powerful Hanseatic League, the economic alliance formed to oversee business among England, Germany, Denmark, Norway, and Sweden. Out on the streets, locals mingled with court officers, tax collectors, pardoners, lawyers, musicians, sailors, bankers, and merchants who spoke Dutch, French, German, and Cornish as priests walked by, crucifixes dangling from cinctured waists.

The town's artisanal manufacturers sold their goods at Lynn's open-air Saturday market, held near the imposing Guildhall of the Holy Trinity, which sat right across from St. Margaret's. It housed the powerful merchants' guild that Margery's father also helped run. It oversaw Lynn's trade and helped fund its rich religious culture.

St. Nicholas Chapel sat about six hundred yards away in north Lynn, one of two chapels of ease to St. Margaret's. Near St. Nicholas's, shoppers could go to Tuesday market, which opened close to the waterfront where ships docked to unload cargo. Packhorses pulled wagons loaded with goods down the main highway, Damgate, as roosters, lambs, goats, and dogs milled about. Public latrines sat at the west end of St. Margaret's.

When a chaplain at St. Margaret's checked the yellow clock in the sky and rang the church bell at 7 A.M., the shops opened. Anything the Kempes and their friends could want was for sale: cakes, pies, gingerbread, biscuits and bread, butter, milk, eggs, damson plum jam, figs, currants, honey, maple ginger sweets, sugar loaves, royal paste of flour and sugar, pistachio nuts, sunflower or caraway seeds, cinnamon, nutmeg, cloves, cardamom, peppercorns, apples, pears, turnips, onions, peas, and cabbage.

At the fish stalls, they scrutinized tables piled high with baskets of oysters, crabs, lobsters, conger eels, lampreys, and herring, as well as fresh trout, cod, sea bream, plaice, turbot, sturgeon, pike, perch, mackerel, sea bass, and blue whiting.

The townspeople haggled with merchants over candles, lamp oil, salt sold from the local salt works, needles, and wool sold by locals. They negotiated with importers who sold kitchenware, bed coverlets, purses and hats just in from Bruges, Flanders cloths, such as linens, velvet, satin, damask, silk, and sarcenet, as well as furs of rabbits, kids, foxes, or squirrels. Other merchants sold timber, such as imported fir boards from places like Norway.

Shoppers could buy rosewater, civet lavender, violets, and ambergris at the perfumers' shops, as well as whitening cosmetics and small round mirrors, combs, scissors, and tweezers. Nearby were dozens of jewelers' shops and goldsmiths. Blacksmiths worked across town in grimy shops hunched over whetstones clanging metal, their fires belching fumes and sparks.

The friends often crossed paths with Guy, a sly, amoral butcher who habitually summoned feelings of sympathy only for himself, and Guy's friend Gilbert, a human block of a skinner who spontaneously triggered panic in all he met. Guy was a pigeon-chested fellow who sweated a lot and whose fish eyes had the frenetic, sidelong look of a man up to something. He believed he was smarter than everyone else, which aggravated his natural mean streak. Like his red-haired, put-upon wife, Ruth, he fancied himself a student of human beings and doubted everything.

Guy worked on Butchers Lane in a shop stacked with raw meat, amid the rhythmic clickety-clack of meat axes, knives, pokers, tongs, grappling hooks, harness rings, kettles, and trivets. Gilbert worked nearby in Skinners Row, getting hides from Guy to sell to the saddlers, shoemakers, booksellers, and tailors in the presence of inspectors in a house on the Common Staith.

Watery ditches were dug in the middle or on the sides of streets on the outskirts of Bishop's Lynn, where, depending on the section, household garbage like mutton bones, oyster shells, and fish skeletons, even whole dinner plates, were often thrown from second-story windows to land among the dead cats or dogs, which were cleaned up by the locals hired by the town.

Thieves and drunkards could be seen reeling down slovenly alleyways toward taverns here, Lynn's main garbage dump on the Ouse in the distance, the filthy effluent running off into waterways. All manner of diseases nestled and thrived in these shadowy corners of England's towns, hunkering down with the fleas and lice that rich and poor picked at and flicked away.

Sailors returning from the North Sea sat in Lynn's alehouses drinking, eating beef pies or tearing at dried salted fish and cheese on bread as they scared the locals with stories from places far away, Jerusalem, Egypt, Constantinople, Persia, India, and China. They told of murdered saints and martyred knights, of fire-breathing dragons, unicorns, forest monsters with giant tusks, and large, gap-toothed behemoths told of in Job 40:15–24, creatures that were really alligators, rhinoceroses, razor-backed hogs, and hippopotamuses. They spoke in hushed tones of a place in Rome where hell below regularly broke forth on land, volcanoes breathing molten fire to swallow Christians.

Margery's father was so good and effective governing Lynn, he was elected mayor five times and to Parliament six times as one of Lynn's two representatives, serving under King Edward III and King Richard II. With a head for numbers and an aptitude for swift, objective decisions, Brunham adjudicated the lingua franca of trade, currency disputes, as well as fights over bonded warehouses and import duties, his back stiffening if anyone played him the fool over who was on the take and who wasn't.

If he wasn't administering royal mandates and governing trading, Brunham was dealing with the militant Henry Le Despenser, bishop of Norwich, who oversaw the town for the church. Powerful soldier-bishops like Despenser collected tithes and stopped heresies, earning the annual salary of an earl.

Brunham also protected the town from possible marine invasion by France and met regularly with visiting royals. Kings Richard II, Henry IV, and Henry V all traveled through Bishop's Lynn. So, too, did the brutal, suspicious Archbishop of Canterbury, Thomas Arundel, orthodox head of the Catholic Church in England who sat next to the seat of power. Royals often came demanding answers to life's problems from the famous local astronomer, Nicholas of Lynn, always frustrated with the unceasing indifference of the stars.

As Margery's parents busied themselves with the town's affairs, their daughter's vivid imagination opened up to the Christian faith. Church, pageant plays, or itinerant preachers were the only entertainment. The Dominicans, Austin friars, Carmelites, and Franciscans, otherwise known as the Grey Friars, were the town's confessors, counselors, preachers, and teachers.

The Brunhams sat in their pew at Mass and listened as friars rolled out stories that became more vivid and gruesome in the retelling.

Saints flayed, saints beheaded, saints crucified upside down. The seven deadly sins semaphored in stories of villainous murderers and pagan tyrants. All were penultimate to the greatest story ever told, Christ's victory over Satan and an earthly world.

During Mass on the feast of Corpus Christi, the first Sunday after Pentecost, a young Margery looked up in wonderment as the priests intoned, "Holy Strong One, Holy Immortal One, Salvator." The Brunhams knelt with the congregation and people outside on the street as the Lynn Corpus Christi guild marched up the center aisle of St. Margaret's behind priests swinging incense around the Blessed Sacrament held high, encased in a lavish, gold monstrance bedazzled in fiery gems.

One Saturday after the feast of Corpus Christi, the Brunhams sat down to a dinner of lobsters in saffron and apples. Her father then read aloud from the family Bible, as Margery played with her pewter figurines of saints, knights, and silver birds in little birdcages. Later, her mother put Margery to bed, sat down next to her and opened her bestiary in her lap, a picture book of morality fables starring forest animals, and then her little red book of saints.

Margery sat transfixed, wide-eyed, as her mother told her about the tragic, heroic tales of the little virgin Agnes martyred for refusing to be married, wanting to only be with Jesus. Or St. Barbara, tortured for her Christianity at the behest of her tyrant father, her breasts cut off, her father beheading her. He was then struck by lightning, reduced to ashes, her mother said.

"Come, Margery, recite," her father ordered, as visiting nobles from London sat at table waiting. Her parents could already see their young daughter had a sharp and retentive memory.

Margery knelt and began, "The ruler of Antioch, Olibrius, martyred the patron saint of our beloved church, St. Margaret, virgin undefiled, because she refused to renounce her Christianity."

Seeing his daughter hesitating, her father commanded, his tone tinged with possessive, parental dread, "Continue."

Margery recited, "While St. Margaret was in prison, Olibrius fed her to Satan in the form of a dragon. But St. Margaret escaped when the cross she carried irritated the dragon's insides and he burst open, praise God."

Her mother said, "Just like Jonah and the whale."

Margery repeated, "Just like Jonah and the whale."

Their friends laughed and clapped, as her parents glowed with delight. "Go outside, Margery," her mother said gently, and she took her dolls out in front of her family's stone and timber house, sculpted cusps adorning its walls outside. Highly observant, Margery studied the comings and goings. There was much to see because England was on edge, profoundly uneasy.

CHAPTER SIX

Turmoil

The fourteenth century was a dazzling time in England, of hero knights and kings, crusades and tournaments. A time of Christian mystics wide open to the extraordinary, when visionaries claimed God and Jesus talked to them, of lush, religious literature separate from the Bible filled with wonderment and vulnerable warmth. The earth was flat, heaven above, hell below, and the pope dominated all of Christianity.

Yet it was one of the most barbaric periods in England's history, wracked by harrowing suffering and death, a violent, hellish time as magical as malign that saw the country's social order upended for good.

Up until 1300, the monarchy was generally stable. But in the fourteenth century, not just one, but two kings were dethroned and allegedly assassinated. First, King Edward II in 1327, and then King Richard II in 1399, overthrown by his cousin, the crusader and Holy Land pilgrim King Henry IV, a ground-breaking leader who overthrew a tyrant only to grab total power for himself in the face of constant revolts.

Meanwhile, the Roman Catholic Church was split asunder by a debilitating papal schism in 1378. Eventually, three popes battled for the Throne of Peter, undermining Pope Boniface VIII's grandiose dream earlier in the century of a religious superpower that would oversee not just Christendom, but all of the kings and emperors in every country on the planet.

The militancy of the Catholic Church in England intensified, manifesting in a meddlesome bureaucracy that saw threats to its power in every corner, in every whisper of reform. The church in England turned itself into a self-aggrandizing fortress, creating laws through its own consistory courts to make its decisions unassailable. It claimed its oaths of loyalty to pope ranked higher than its oaths to the kings of England, that its powers of taxation through tithing were separate from the monarchy's power to tax, and anyone who withheld tithes would be excommunicated. Because they were educated, the clergy also exercised power as civil servants, in the diplomatic services, the secular courts, and the exchequer's office as moneychangers and accountants.

Church leaders accepted from the rich and poor tithes of land, money, food, even farm animals, as they steadily increased their personal ownership of property. The church owned an estimated one-third of England's real estate. English peasants often were required to spend much of their week working for no pay for the Catholic Church in England. A church marbled through with the fat of corruption soon became a financial drain on England.

As the church unleashed an infantry of functionaries to defend itself, behind the scenes, its clergy steadily deconsecrated it. Many clerics enjoyed an indolent lifestyle, with lavish feasts and concubinages, secret marriages where children were passed off as nephews or nieces. Plenty of material for Geoffrey Chaucer, author of *The Canterbury Tales*, the most famous writer of this period.

Meanwhile, the pope had relocated from Rome to Avignon, France, in 1309, underscoring tensions that exploded in 1337 in the Hundred Years War. King Edward III laid claim to the French throne—*honi soit qui mal y pense*, "shamed be he who thinks evil of it." The pope in Avignon increasingly sent scores of bureaucrats into England and beyond to collect money for the no-longer "Roman" Catholic Church. Papal pardons sold at a discount when business was slow, the roads of England already plowed through by local clergy—along with Venetian bankers with usurious loans for the monarchy.

English gentry and peasantry alike grew increasingly furious that they were subsidizing the tyranny of a mysterious French pope backed by a French crown constantly interfering in their affairs, a grievance deeply rooted in the national psyche. Slowly, England became a country greening with its own ambitions, its own separate identity.

Parliament first passed an early version of the statute of praemunire in 1351, which said no authority, not even the king, had the right to subject England and its church to any foreign power, including the pope. It came about two centuries before King Henry VIII used this same law to break away from the Roman Catholic Church for good. In 1362, King Edward III became the first monarch to address Parliament in English, and a law was enacted ordering the use of English as the official language of the country, supplanting French.

But then the worst happened. Through the streets of England had come storms, flood, famine, and war. But now something more terrible had arrived, a colossus more lethal than anything anyone had ever seen. Like an ancient specter, it came from nowhere. Then suddenly, it was everywhere. With shocking speed, the Great Pestilence systematically ripped through an utterly defenseless population in Europe, beginning in 1347. In just four years' time, this colossal besom of annihilation swept a great swath of the population from the soil. Scholars estimate that by 1400, the bubonic plague drove the earth's population down from an estimated 443 million to 350 million.

It was so infectious, it nearly killed everyone, and it's an enduring mystery why it didn't. People of all ages and from all walks of life dropped like bumble bees on a harvest day. Fear flew like spores through a desperate population seeking comfort in a church in apocalyptic overdrive to terrify the people into virtue, that the plague was God's just punishment on a faithless land.

"Or maybe it was a trepidation in the spheres," explained the nervous doctors of the University of Paris along with astrologers to an outraged King Philip VI of France. "A devilish miasma created by a lethal triple conjunction of Saturn, Jupiter, and Mars in the fortieth degree of Aquarius, which sucked up ocean waters into a poisonous death cloud." That was the medieval logic of the time, the answers as remote as Jupiter. They may as well have been sorting through chicken entrails like the Roman augurs.

In reality, it was a cargo of bacteria, *Yersinia pestis,* incubating in the bellies of fleas hitching a ride on the bodies of rats and other animals scurrying aboard trade ships and caravans from central Asia. An outbreak of bubonic plague worsened when it was accompanied by pneumonic plague, possibly bringing a string of different diseases to fruition, like a mutation of cattle murrain.

It was called the Black Death because of the black buboes it created, swelling to the size of an orange. Necks, armpits, and groins literally swelled into dark mounds, and death came within days, even hours.

The Great Plague set upon England in 1349, remorselessly slicing the population in half, scholars estimate. The plague abated by 1351, but recurred repeatedly through ensuing decades, dropping the median lifespan to twenty-one years.

In the fields outside Bishop's Lynn, the sick along with the healthy worked in the slate-grey twilight rooting out old parsnips and cabbage, plucking at what wool was left on sheep to sell, England's main export. Starving pigs and goats on the sides of the roads scrounged for food, tumulus piles of the newly dead in the distance. "Nature has turned on itself," a farmer said to his friend.

The countryside was emptied. Families abandoned huts where parents had frantically bivouacked their homes by stacking broken furniture on their thresholds, believing they could stop the ingress of the fatal disease. Remaining villagers gathered at open doors, hands empty, wondering at what news any visitors might be bringing, as children stood behind in a foot of water or collapsed in corners. All of them exhausted, their souls shaken night and day. Peasants poured into towns like Bishop's Lynn, ravaged and uncouth, a diorama of the failure of the feudal system now smack in the townspeople's faces.

A worker shortage took hold. Remaining laborers grew enraged at the court's decision to fix wages at a set level. Fields and groves lay ignored, untended. Meanwhile, unfinanced wars and mismanagement had emptied the royal treasury. Banks then crashed around the world after a credit bubble burst in the money center Florence. Credit evaporated, real estate values plunged, and, given the death and destruction, people spent their savings like there was no tomorrow.

Soon, England was hit with its worst tax rebellion in its history, the murderous Peasants' Revolt in 1381, triggered by a series of three intolerable poll taxes on people as young as teenagers. The church was exempt. Tinder dry, the countryside exploded. Public order collapsed.

A moving hive of peasants swarmed from town to town, burning down homes and offices, murdering many. The peasants torched buildings in London, including Lambeth Palace, seat of the head of the church, and the Savoy, the palace of John of Gaunt, son of Edward III and father to Henry IV. The peasants also stormed into the chambers of King Richard II's mother, Joan, the Fair Maid of Kent, said to have passed out from shock.

Then the peasants did the unthinkable. Somehow they broke into England's intimidating citadel, the impregnable Tower of London, and beheaded the sixty-five-year-old leader of the church, the Archbishop of Canterbury, Simon of Sudbury, incompetently taking up to nine whacks at his neck. The teenage Henry Bolingbroke, later King Henry IV, is thought to have escaped the intense rioting after a knight hid him in a cupboard in the Tower.

The Peasants' Revolt fell apart after one of its leaders, the insolent Wat Tyler, was stabbed to death at a meeting with the fourteen-year-old King Richard II in Smithfield. In Margery's hometown area, Henry le Despenser, nicknamed "Episcopus Martius," or the "fighting bishop" of Norwich, won praise for squashing a local rebellion led by the dyer Geoffrey Litster, beheading him and executing his followers.

All along, the rise of the mercantilist was upon the land. It was a new day; the people could carve out their own destinies. Out of the destruction was born a new social stratum: the doubting middle class, unleashing robust economic forces like never before.

They first arose in the environs of England's great universities, Oxford and Cambridge, and then in the countryside, villages thrusting into new towns and cities. The chaos and death had brought out a singular English instinct, ordinary people revealed a country to itself. A no-nonsense, commonsense logic that rang like a bell, tinctured by a perverse, independent mind-set, which finally picked the lock on a Bible hidden like a secret treasure chest for centuries. It was as if they suddenly found themselves stumbling around in the dark of their bedrooms, everything different, strange.

The people took note how the clergy blamed the Black Death on the very same vices they themselves practiced. That despite all their boasts about prophecies, no one in the church foretold the plague. People also took note of a grubby vacuousness, how their hard-earned coins quickly vanished into the pockets of church pardoners like something out of *Ali Baba and the Forty Thieves*.

Slowly, reform was carried on the wind from town to town. But since order and freedom cannot occupy the same space, church and state panicked. An uneasiness swept across England and encroached upon Bishop's Lynn.

CHAPTER SEVEN

Neighbors Mock

Along with the new middle class came John and Margery Kempe, caught up in the crosscurrents of a modern age. After marrying in 1393, the couple moved into a tenement house John owned in the center of town. John was eventually elected one of the town's treasurers. But the booming and busting local economy was still weak. They and their friends struggled to get their footing.

Against John's wishes, Margery started a brewery, hanging a bushel on a pole above the door of their home showing freshly brewed ale was for sale. "Margery, you have no experience of it," John warned calmly as he could. But Margery replied tersely, "I can do it." John sighed; again he would have to wait until all of his wife's emotions rushed past to talk sense into her.

After four years the business fell apart. The froth on the ale suddenly went flat, a stuck fermentation. Embarrassed, her workers quit, and the young couple's finances were a shambles. Margery meekly said as they stood in their now-shuttered brewery, "John, I should have followed your counsel. My pride is to blame. I will fix with a good will where I have trespassed."

Margery poured money and energy into a fragile new endeavor, milling. She hired a man and two horses to turn the grindstones to pulverize corn into meal. But soon that business fell apart, too. John and Margery struggled to find a business that wasn't a money sink and that would give them purpose and pleasure, as Margery began to believe her business failures were Jesus calling her from foolish pride.

Locals grew jealous of Margery, an innate pettiness that overwhelmed their Christianity. "Not even a horse would work for Margery now," Ruth muttered to Gilbert's hulking wife, Mathilda, as they watched the Kempes and their children walking to market.

"Fortune has turned her wheel against the Kempes, their humility just a pretense to their pride," Mathilda whispered back.

Overhearing them as he walked by, Fr. Donald, an owlish local friar staying with Margery's confessor, Fr. Spryngolde, turned their gossiping into a teachable moment, "Vanity turns all to sorrow in the end, Caesarius of Arles warned," as Ruth chuckled.

Years passed. As Margery walked to market each week, children in tow, she often thought of the swirling, watercolor vision of Jesus she had had years before. She dwelled on the death Jesus chose, and cried in public. John tried to console her, as Margery became increasingly convinced, as many Christians believed, that the way to avoid purgatory was by experiencing suffering on earth.

"Persecution is the fate of the true Christian; it brings us closer to Jesus," she told John.

But John worried, "How are we going to feed our growing family?"

One night, as John quietly slept, Margery lay in bed restless, her senses heightened. Then suddenly, off in the distance came a strange sound. "What was that?" Margery asked the darkness.

An otherworldly melody, a silvery concord between heaven's orchestra and earth below had somehow reached her ears. It would be music Margery claimed to hear off and on for another twenty-five years, to the point where it blocked out entire conversations. Suddenly, Margery was one with the universe, just as she had felt years before. Thrilled, she jumped out of bed, awakening John by shouting, "I must be in paradise." Margery explained as John rubbed his eyes, "Alas, that ever I sinned. It is full merry in heaven."

Whenever Margery heard this melody, she would cry, in church, out on the streets, at home or in the fields, as cows quietly looked back chewing over mossy, stone fences, and neighbors looked at each other. She would also feel the sudden urge to go to church, getting up to go at three in the morning to walk the few blocks from their house to St. Margaret's where local monks were already saying lauds, the first office of the day. Margery would stay there praying and crying as the early dawn poured gold through the church's eastern windows, even into the afternoon, not breaking for midday supper.

"Margery is now blessed with holy tears, just like Marie d'Oignies and St. Bridget," Master Alan, a Carmelite friar, explained to Fr. Spryngolde. Meanwhile, her husband patiently tried to excuse her sobbing. "Hearing angel musicians again?" William teased. Back home, John pleaded, "Please, Margery, don't chastise our friends to leave things of the earth behind. They don't hear what you hear, they don't understand."

What the townspeople didn't understand was that, to Margery, to weep was to pray, her sobs were simply another form of prayer sent to heaven. What the locals also couldn't understand was that Margery couldn't help her visions. She swore they came unbidden, as gentle as a touch on the shoulder or like a bird suddenly bursting out of a fireplace to fly around a living room.

One night, Margery and John sat at the dinner table with their friends in the home of Catherine and Thomas. Talk at the table turned to doings in town. "St. Margaret's needs a new roof because rain is leaking through. Fr. Spryngolde forbids even the ringing of the church bell," Catherine said at the table. "Fr. Donald is asking us to increase our tithes."

Eleanor grew annoyed, "Perhaps he can leave off buying mutton since he has gone pear-shaped and so has his Christianity."

Suddenly, Margery heard the ancient melodies and blurted out her favorite non sequitur, "It is full merry in heaven." Flabbergasted, Catherine said across the table as she passed a bottle of ale, her freckled face turned peevish, "Why do you talk so of the joy that is in heaven? You don't know it and you haven't been there any more than we have."

Eleanor chided, "You always do tend to take yourself so very high." Margery looked into her lap, feeling awkward, out of place, as if she was always laughing at the wrong time.

But the rebuke upset the usually placid William. He loved Margery; he understood her. His wife Eleanor had married him because "he's like taking a warm bath, warm as a tavern," she had confided to Catherine. "But when he gets mad, watch out."

Now William was furious. "Leave her alone, Eleanor," he said. "'A heart at peace gives life to the body, but envy is the rotten corpse draped on the bones.' Proverbs 14:30. A kind heart creates kindness, a jealous heart, jealousy, an evil heart, evil."

Eleanor asked, "Who said that last part?"

William replied, "I did. That was me," as his wife giggled.

Throughout, Margery smiled wanly as John sat bent over his dinner plate. William leaned over and said to him, "Wherever there is a human being, there is a chance for kindness. That is Margery now." Eleanor joked, "And a chance for correcting, too," as her husband frowned.

Later, when the party was over, Catherine said tartly as they left, "I thank you for a most unusual evening," and they all walked home.

Margery's soul was now on fire for God, a soul in love that only desired to live wholly in God's presence. She increased her confessions, upping them to three times a day. She also began to fast constantly, skipping meals.

At home, it dawned on John that his wife might be appropriating the words of church hymns she hummed at home as if they were her own inner history. She furtively sewed a piece of tough sacking cloth used to dry malt for ale on the inside of her shift, hiding her new hair shirt from her husband even while bearing more children. "What are those red marks on your back?" John asked, suspicious.

He buried his face in his hands as Doctor Gunther told him the unfortunate news in the doctor's office in town. "Margery is dying from St. Anthony's fire, ergotism. She got it from working in your brewery. That explains her convulsions. Her limbs will fall off. She has eight months to live," he said.

"It's from a hair shirt, you idiot. Your practice has one week to live," Catherine yelled as she marched in, as the doctor cowered.

Meanwhile, the malicious circle of criticism cinched tighter around Margery, as people made fun of her behind her back. "Margery has gone mad again," Ruth whispered to Mathilda, contributing to the growing consensus about Margery in Bishop's Lynn.

"She is ruining her family's good name with such peculiar behavior," Mathilda muttered back.

But their attacks only made Margery happier, infuriating the gossips. Suffering would not sap her will, it would strengthen it. The greater the rejection, the more she threw herself into the arms of the church, growing happier than when she lived in the dignity of high society.

"I am happy when I am mocked for our Lord's love, just as all the apostles, martyrs, and all those who ever came to heaven by the way of tribulation," she explained to Fr. Spryngolde. "Mockery is proof I have sinned greatly against God. I am worthy of more shame and sorrow than any man could do to me. The way of scorn and contempt in this world is the right way to heaven, for Christ himself chose that way."

Week after week, with pendulum-like regularity, Margery cried at Mass as she looked up at the Man of Sorrows hanging on the cross, Jesus who was never in the abstract, always real, always nearby. Margery loudly grieved for her own sins, for all of her unkind behaviors to God and to others even as far back as childhood.

"Be silent woman," Ruth's husband Guy hissed at Margery as he and his wife sat behind the Kempes in church, even though Guy could care less about the liturgy. He just liked to use the public latrine outside.

"Margery could cry a brewery," Ruth joked to Guy as the Kempes walked by with their children out the church door at the end of Mass.

Catherine shot back, "Being petty doesn't make you important."

Guy retorted, "She should sit and spin and stop preaching spiritual things."

A couple of days later at market, Guy continued his usual practice of overcharging for rank meat left too long on hooks in the midday sun, ignoring Thomas's suggestions to buy his salt as a preservative. Guy's modus vivendi was to cheat, deceive, and do as little as possible. "Tight as the skin of a drum," Thomas said to William as he pushed back his flopping hair.

Ruth advised customers who complained about her husband's rotten meat, "Just add pepper or parsley to the sauce, you won't taste a thing."

Although a comforting watchtower at market, a professional sampler thrusting her nose in the wares like a gourmand, Ruth despised the way neighbors pitied Margery, loathing more those who pitied her. She soon found a new line of attack. Margery had an authenticity gap. Her crying was so instantaneous, it seemed confected, mechanical. "Don't you agree that Margery can summon her sobbing at will?" Ruth asked one morning at market, eyebrows tweezed high.

Guy stopped chopping beef and thought, not Margery the delusional, but Margery the opportunist. "Aren't you a bit harsh on your own sex," he replied as he turned back to chopping.

The next day, a sparkling Sunday morning dawned. It was Advent, an early snow packed in window corners started to melt under the cold sun. But Fr. Donald was annoyed. The priests said Mass in Latin with their backs to the congregation and couldn't control parishioners who wandered in and out, got in rowdy fights in the pews, chatted, laughed at jokes, or played with dice.

But as the altar boys rang the Sanctus bells, Fr. Donald stood distracted, thinking of a lyric he had been working on for his own Book of Hours, "the flowery sky music of majestic priestly choirs," which no one would read because the language was remarkably insipid. He held the Blessed Host only at elbow height during the sacring, not above his head as he was supposed to, the congregation miffed at this indifferent priest in an already indifferent universe.

"Hold it up, hold it up, I want to see my Maker," a man yelled. Catherine whispered to Eleanor, "Eucharist is invalidated by a man lacking in grace." Fr. Donald then hissed to his assisting cleric Friar Oliver, "If they are not looking up at the Eucharist, they are Lollards. Get their names."

Meanwhile, Margery fought to keep her passionate love for God bottled up, but that only made it worse. Unable to contain herself, she gasped, "Jesus, I die for you. I love you," and fell prostrate to the floor of the center aisle at St. Margaret's.

"She is at her invention again," Ruth muttered to Guy as she looked at Margery as if she had just smelled feet. John then stoically took his grieving wife by the elbow down the center aisle.

"You are interrupting Holy Mass, Margery," Fr. Donald chastised her outside church, arms folded under his robe. "You look like a fool, you blubber like Balaam's ass."

Sour-lipped, Ruth and Guy had followed the Kempes out the front door. "You can leave off crying when you want. You just weep for attention," Ruth chided. "You're nothing but a fake alabaster saint who will cry herself into a puddle of clay."

Guy agreed, "You, with your preachings, telling us how to live. You're a vile Lollard meddling in the church."

Margery whirled around. "Please, don't," John whispered, eyes beseeching.

Margery agreed, and whispered back, "The more slander and reproof that I suffer, the more I shall increase in grace and in devotion." So the Kempes ignored Ruth and Guy and walked home.

Back at the rectory, the table topic turned to Margery. "Rather exuberant today," said Fr. Donald as they sat down to lunch. Even though he put on a show of being the town's favorite nice fellow, oafishly backslapping fellow clerics in a phony show of comity, he would roar like Boudicca when frustrated over the tiniest of things, "It is God's will I yell at you."

Friar Oliver offered, "Maybe the right ventricle of her brain is ill."

A young priest chuckled, "Why didn't we become anchorites?"

Fr. Donald said, "Errare humanum est, perseverare diabolicum."

As they stared back mystified, impatient, he said, "To err is human; to persist in erring is diabolical. The devil knows each man's weakness and tempts him accordingly. Margery's is vanity."

But Friar Oliver said as he rubbed his jaw, now sore with a toothache after gargling with wine for three days, "Leave her be."

Fr. Donald shot back, "After you pray to St. Apollonia, why don't you rub unicorn oil on your jaw and boil the shadow of that sparrow out the window and gargle with that." Then he handed Friar Oliver a glass of salt water.

As the months turned into summer, Margery found she could endure longer fasts, whittling her body down to nothing. Increasingly shunned in Bishop's Lynn, Margery now feared no devil in hell, but instead grew afraid she loved God more than he loved her.

Then more temptation struck at her weakest point, her old sin, which Margery thought she had rubbed out with her hair shirt. Walking outside St. Margaret's before evensong one day in late July, a young man Margery had grown particularly fond of said, "For anything, I would lie by your side, and you would not be able to resist me." Margery was filled with desire to the point where she couldn't say her prayers. Worse, they were flirting on the feast day of the patron saint of Bishop's Lynn's church, the virgin martyr St. Margaret of Antioch. Fr. Donald saw them talking, frowned, and took note.

Feeling like God had abandoned her, a few days later Margery confided to the young man that he could, in fact, have his way with her. But he alarmed her by quickly backing away, perhaps realizing the illicit thrill of flirtation was low-grade adultery. "Why, no Margery, you misunderstood me," he said. "It would be better if I was chopped as small as meat for the pot than to be with you."

Guilt compounded Margery's feelings of loneliness, she sat abandoned in empty chapels, her life in limbo. Society's doors were shutting, even as she was being shown the key to open every door.

CHAPTER EIGHT

1408

*O*ne of the worst cold spells in living memory was just now leaving the land. Animals died by the thousands, ink froze in inkpots, and even the salty ocean waves partly iced over. The townspeople would remember this deep freeze for the rest of their lives.

As she knelt at the cathedral, Margery wept for forgiveness, praying her husband would agree to chastity. Jesus suddenly came to her in an astonishing vision, "You shall never come into hell nor into purgatory, but when you pass out of this world, within the twinkling of an eye, you shall have the bliss of heaven, for I am the same God who has brought your sins to mind and caused you to be shriven of them. And I grant you contrition until your life's end."

Margery sat bolt upright, transfixed. Jesus continued, "You have a hair-shirt on your back. I want you to leave off wearing it, and I shall give you a hair-shirt in your heart which shall please me much more than all the hair-shirts in the world."

Jesus also ordered, "You must give up that which you love best in this world, and that is the eating of meat," ordering Margery instead to receive the Eucharist every Sunday. This last request would trigger resentment, as churchgoers typically received communion once annually at Easter. As she walked home from church, Margery, worried, asked Jesus what she should think about. Jesus comforted her, "Think of my mother."

In a Jacob's ladder of a vision, Margery saw the "Holy Kinship," the Holy Family's circle of relatives where six of the twelve apostles were cousins to Jesus, because Jesus's mother Mary had two half-sisters, Mary Cleopas and Mary Salome. In her vision she went back in time and helped St. Anne tend to Mary as a baby girl, even joining an older Mary and her husband Joseph to visit Mary's pregnant cousin Elizabeth, mother of John the Baptist, bearing wine sweetened with honey and spices.

Fr. Donald suspiciously eyed Margery as she later talked at market at length about the Gospels, the turbine of his thumbs rotating over. He finally marched up and angrily chastised her, "It is against the law to teach the Bible."

But Margery disobeyed him, as she would time and again. "The Gospel gives me leave to speak of God," she retorted. Fr. Donald watched Margery walk away. "I shall stop her soon enough," he thought.

Later, on a Friday before Pentecost, Margery sat after Mass in St. Margaret's Church, praying quietly as remaining parishioners huddled against each other for warmth. Winter would not let go of the land. Her husband was home with the children. Her neighbors Ruth and Mathilda eyed her expectantly.

The parishioners were startled out of their seats by a loud crack from up above. Panicked, congregants ran to the side aisles. But Margery stayed in her seat praying, her head deep into her picture Book of Hours. "Maybe this is God's judgment finally come upon Margery," joked Ruth. Margery heard her, and feared the same.

"Or maybe upon you and I for thinking that," admonished Mathilda. Suddenly, a huge beam of wood and cement broke free from the highest point in the ceiling above, plummeted down and clobbered Margery on her back, a blow that would have killed

Hercules. Thinking she was going to die, Margery whispered, "Jesus, mercy."

John Wyreham, a fabric dealer and neighbor, ran to Margery's side, fearing she was dead. Seeing her eyes were shut tightly, he gently pulled on her sleeve and asked, "How are you feeling, ma'am?" A crowd gathered, morbidly afraid. Seconds ticked by.

But then Margery suddenly sat up, nothing broken. She had called on Jesus and he had protected her. She had no pain whatsoever. "I thank you for your kindness, John," Margery said as he helped her to her feet. The parishioners stepped back, awed by this human dynamo. "You should be dead, if not lame, and yet you are neither. This is a miracle," Wyreham said, as churchgoers agreed.

Ruth disagreed, "No, it is God's wrath." Fr. Donald folded his arms under his cloak and walked away, preferring to remain at a reserve from the others.

News shot through the town, reaching All Saints Church in South Lynn, where Master Alan sat reading. The townspeople looked up to him. He was a man of stature, later a doctor of divinity at Cambridge University, his library shelves creaking. If a man of such skeptical intelligence believed in Margery, then her credibility would increase. "You must come see this miracle, Master Alan," a friar rushed up to him, excited.

Master Alan raced to the church, pulled the beam from a bonfire outside that a warden had lit to keep warm, and weighed the masonry. His verdict: Nine pounds total, increasing exponentially in weight due to the drop. "It's a great miracle. Our Lord is highly magnified for the preserving of this creature against the malice of her enemies," he told the assembled crowd, who stood, mouths agape, staring back at Margery. Margery, however, was walking away, lost in prayer. She had a bigger problem on her mind.

CHAPTER NINE

Marriage in Trouble

For years Margery had struggled in her marriage as her faith grew. Things became steadily worse for her husband. While they were in bed on a Wednesday evening in Easter week, John rolled on top of Margery, hoping for payment of his marital debt. But Margery lay stiff as a board, saying repeatedly to the ceiling, "Jesus, help me."

All John could do was roll back over, a lid capping his ardor. Later, he turned again to Margery, merely hoping for a good night kiss. The only exposed area he could find was the private, white skin of her inner ankle. He kissed her hairline behind her ear.

According to the law, John owned his wife, just the same as if he owned domestic animals like cows or horses. He could order Margery to do what he wanted because under church law, spouses owed a marital debt of sex to each other, even though the church, too, paradoxically forbade sex during all sorts of times, giving John's plight an added piquancy.

Humans were incapable of controlling their sexual desires, St. Augustine had warned centuries earlier, so the church had to step in. Only propagation of the species entitled human beings to the act of making love without sin. As such, the Catholic Church prohibited intercourse during a head-spinning multiplicity of times: feast days, Wednesdays, Fridays, and Sundays, during menstruation, pregnancy, or nursing, even during daylight.

Nightly John made the epic journey to Margery, climbing confident into their bed, looking forward to their next adventure in the soft, carnal darkness. Nightly, Margery resisted. One evening, as she and John lay in bed, Margery thought, "The debt of matrimony is so abominable to me, I would rather drink the ooze and muck in the gutter."

If John was going to have his way, she wouldn't be present for it. Margery finally said, "I may not deny you my body, but all the love and affection of my heart is withdrawn from all earthly creatures and set on God alone."

John meekly backed down, saying, "It is good to abstain, but not just yet." Then he thought better of it, sat up and ordered, "I will have my will." So Margery obeyed, cringing and grieving through the act of love, distressed she was displeasing God. When Margery discovered she was pregnant again, conflicted, she told Jesus, "I am not worthy to hear you speak."

But Jesus comforted her, "Rest assured that I love wives also, and especially those wives who would live chaste if they might have their will and do all they can to please me as you do," adding, "for love quenches all sin." That was the answer she needed to hear, as her desire for chastity grew. "Three years I will give you John, and no more," Margery warned.

Meanwhile, Eleanor and Catherine grew increasingly worried about the changes in their friend. "Isn't the act of denying the body an act of sinking more deeply into the body?" Eleanor asked Catherine as they walked to Tuesday market.

"Perhaps it's the first step in dying to one's former self," Catherine replied.

The Kempes continued in their uneasy marriage. Margery spent more time in church. "What is that ghastly ruckus?" neighbors whispered, as Margery loudly sobbed, birds blasting off the church roof en masse. Bishop's Lynn didn't want any more attention from the authorities, having had its own historic battle with heresy.

Years before, one of the town's favorite sons had threatened to turn Lynn into a hotbed of schism. The murderous crackdown shocked England, a backlash that would eventually put Margery's life at risk, too. It all began because of simple things like pilgrimages and relics.

CHAPTER TEN

Backlash

All along, the church's big business of pardons, indulgences, and simony was running full blast. Pope Boniface VIII declared the first Jubilee Year in 1300, when Christians could win forgiveness of all sins so long as they confessed and visited the basilicas of Sts. Peter and Paul in Rome. Jubilees were supposed to happen every hundred years, but then the church announced one in 1350, 1390, and 1423. Christians paid big money for indulgences, which could wipe out even tens of thousands of years in purgatory. Clergy increasingly engaged in religious racketeering, accepting parish dues for confessions, communion, even the chiming of church bells.

"But will the poor go to hell because they can't afford salvation?" Eleanor asked Catherine, who had no response.

Also crucial to the church's cash flow were pilgrimages to holy sites and relics. Churches around the world advertised relics of the Holy Family, the apostles, martyrs, and saints, which could ward off death and drought, find missing people, remove worms from dogs, and bind snakebites. Even though people like Geoffrey Chaucer said they were often just pig or sheep bones.

In the Holy Land, you could see where Jesus was born, where he preached, where he was crucified, and where he was buried. Guides touted slivers of the One True Cross, the Blessed Mother's holy breast milk, barbs from Christ's crown of thorns, clothes from the Virgin Mary's wardrobe, or pieces of the sail of St. Peter's ship.

Popes and kings fought over relics, paying big money to hoard these sacred pieces of salvation. They were showcased in marvelous reliquaries of the finest craftsmanship, concave crosses, extravagant caskets, miniature buildings made of precious gold and silver, studded with gems. Pilgrimages became fashionable. Christians toured the world, up to five times annually, to see relics and holy places. A collecting mania seized Christians in a fever grip of trophy souvenirs, relics, and painted images.

Oxford University's John Wyclif then aimed a blast of realism at church leaders more than a century before Martin Luther, King Henry VIII, and his children King Edward VI and Queen Elizabeth I reformed the church.

Wyclif's North Star was Jesus, his shield the king and common law. The movement this Bible scholar inspired, Lollardy, was uniquely English in its common sense but poison to church leaders whose ability to resist reform proved uncanny.

Wyclif fumed that foreign popes held powerful sway over England, having helped negotiate the curtailment of England's payments to the papacy. He then grew increasingly angry watching church leaders abuse their authority at the expense of ordinary Christians. To Wyclif, the church was blighted by a dark superstition that sold salvation in relics, in worshiping statues, in an accretion of lavish ceremonies and rules.

With his intimidating long beard and piercing eyes, Wyclif thundered that the real church was a community of all Christians who must be allowed to read the Bible on their own. The Gospel mattered more than sacraments, more than popes, and Christ was the head of the church, not the pope.

In treatise after treatise, Wyclif demanded church leaders stop defrauding the faithful and cheapening the divine heritage of the apostles into rank cravenness. Scripture did not support sacraments, including confession to a priest, confession was only owed directly to God, just as the apostles and Mary Magdalene spoke directly to Jesus. Anything else was blasphemous.

Wyclif went even further, roundly declaring there was no basis in scripture for any of the church hierarchy, from priest to pope. Every man and woman without sin was as good as the pope. Wyclif also attacked church corruption, demanding the court liquidate or tax the church's assets and give the proceeds to the poor, just as the court of King Henry II had wanted.

All across England and Europe, Wyclif's ideas caught fire. Lollardy became wildly, dangerously popular. It fractured England's desperately needed unity right smack in the middle of the Hundred Years War. In 1371, two Austin friars shocked the church with a strong case for taxing the clergy before Parliament. In 1376, the court of King Edward III debated a 10 percent tax on the church.

Sympathizers at court were proud of their learned theologian Wyclif, proud that Oxford was a force to be reckoned with internationally. These included John of Gaunt, father to Henry IV, and the nobleman Sir John Oldcastle, member of Parliament and soon a personal friend to King Henry IV and his son King Henry V. Oldcastle later openly entertained Lollards at his home, and they revered him as their military leader, hoping he would lead a coup d'etat. Hearing Satan clicking at his heels, Pope Gregory XI condemned Wyclif's teachings in 1377, and he was repeatedly put on trial, but then set free.

Wyclif then rejected the doctrine of transubstantiation, which said that during Mass the priest had the power to transform bread and wine into the real presence of Jesus's body and blood. Wyclif said that the bread and wine spiritually represented Christ, and only if the priest was true in faith.

Seeing reform was hopeless, Wyclif became radical. The pope was the Antichrist running a church of the damned, he said. But his backers at court rejected him. The pope again condemned Wyclif's teachings in 1382, and Lollardy went underground.

As a severe drought parched the country, Wyclif's followers, Nicholas Hereford and John Purvey, began translating St. Jerome's Bible, the Latin Vulgate, into English, a historic turning point. Oxford University forced Wyclif into retirement, and he died of a stroke in 1384.

In 1393, the year Margery gave birth, members of the Privy Council again touted Wyclif's beliefs before Parliament. Two years later, Lollard dissidents nailed numerous demands, including that the church be liquidated and taxed, to the doors of Westminster Abbey and St. Paul's Cathedral. Soon, Wyclif's teachings would put ordinary Christians in mortal danger—including priests.

CHAPTER ELEVEN

Priest Arrested

A fresh, mid-morning rain tapped on his windowpane, inter-rupting William Sawtrey, pastor of St. Margaret's church in Bishop's Lynn, as he reviewed his Sunday sermon while eating breakfast in his chambers.

Sawtrey had wanted to be a priest since he was a little boy, the church his home away from home. Now in his mid-thirties, he increasingly drew many to his sermons with his refreshing, common-sense take on the Gospels. The Sunday prior, he had stepped into the pulpit deeply upset. Sawtrey had watched the people in Bishop's Lynn struggling with all sorts of problems, the indiscriminate slaughter of war, famine, hurricanes, and the Black Death.

The people were worn-out, tired of everything, tired of each other, tired of hearing that their endless hardship was righteous punishment for sin from a violent God whose vengeance had wiped out entire civilizations like the Canaanites. All had seen too much darkness, which is why they seemed like a bruised congregation now looking up at him with the skeptical, exhausted look of hyper vigilance. Yet Sawtrey believed he could bring them back with the living reality of Jesus's story, a story that felt just as real as if it had happened only yesterday.

"I see your despair. I see you struggling to raise your families through unrelenting pain," Sawtrey said as the parishioners hushed their children and sat back to listen. "I've seen you bury your babies, your spouses, your parents, and grandparents. I even stopped you from jumping into the graves you dug for your beloved dead."

As a man and his wife bent their heads down, fighting back tears, Sawtrey, now angry, said, "I see you come here confused over whether to grieve or to do penance for some mysterious sin that you think brought down God's wrath upon you. Why work? Why even get up out of bed when the worst has happened, when the best has been stolen from you, when priests tell you it is your fault? But still, despite all of this unending grief, you come. You still believe. You still have hope. Just as another man had hope long ago, even though he had no reason to. A man who saw up close another man who claimed he was the Son of God dying on the cross. This man had every reason not to believe Jesus, just as you also have every reason not to believe."

As the parishioners sat up straighter, Sawtrey continued, "Remember this. The first robber doubted Jesus as the three hung on their crosses on Golgotha in the dying afternoon light, facing a setting sun in the west grey in despair, just as you have seen it. The first thief joined in with the Pharisees mocking Jesus, 'Are you not the Messiah? Because if you truly are God, you could come down off of your cross and help us down, too. Then, and only then, will we believe in you.'"

Sawtrey went on, "Only Jesus's loved ones remained. His mother Mary, the Apostle John, and Mary Magdalene were shocked to see the crowd cheering for Jesus's death, horrified to see their faces beaming up at him, wanting him to die, his crown of thorns hurting him more than he would let it show. They were all shattered by a grief they had never known that would drive them to their knees at night. Just as you have grieved."

He added, "I know that terrible times have led you to doubt. But that is not what you do. Just like the crucified second robber, Dismas, his name means the second one. He looked into Jesus's eyes at his loneliest hour. Dismas was closer to Jesus than his own mother."

The congregation was now electrified. Sawtrey continued, "Ask yourselves, why should Dismas believe in Jesus? It didn't make any sense. Here was a man claiming he was God, but he was dying on the cross next to him. Dismas knew he was a terrible sinner. Why should he hope for even a shred of kindness? But did Dismas join in mocking the dying Redeemer? We teach you the Gospels. What does the Gospel of Luke say?"

Unsure, a man in the seventh row on the side said, "He scolded the other robber: 'Have you no fear of God? We deserve this, but he did nothing wrong.'" Sawtrey waited.

A woman behind him timidly ventured, "He then said to Jesus, 'Lord, remember me when you come into your kingdom.'"

Sawtrey teared up in gratitude, "Perfect. That is exactly what Dismas said. He turned to Jesus and said simply 'Lord.' Not 'if you are Lord,' or, 'as you call yourself Lord.' Simply, 'Lord.' With the faith of a child, Dismas saw that Jesus was the Son of God and he believed. Because Dismas believed, because he didn't abandon Jesus, Jesus in his immortal kindness told Dismas he would follow him that day into paradise, the second one."

Sawtrey fought back tears as he comforted the congregation now crying, "Just as you to this day never abandoned Jesus, each other, or your faith. Because you love and believe, just as Dismas loved and believed."

Then Sawtrey smiled and said as his voice broke, "And that is why Jesus will always remember you."

As the parishioners wiped away tears, Sawtrey knelt, put his hands over his face, and quietly prayed, "*In te domino confido non confundar.*" ("In you, Lord, I have put my trust, never let me be put to confusion.")

A few months later, Sawtrey was angrily pacing in his chambers. "Evil distracting fallacies," he said to a cleric.

"What do you mean, good sir," a cleric asked.

Sawtrey said, "That it is just as good to worship wooden relics as it is to follow the word of Christ. Honor only God and Jesus, the Lord of saints, not saints' wooden images or dirty combs or rotting boots and purses, when Jesus has shown us the way to a higher perfection. Man's soul depends only on grace from up above, not from worshiping fake man-made things. And you cannot pay for the church to intervene for your soul as you would the town doctor." The cleric bent and hurried away to Bishop Despenser's manor.

Ruthless and dangerously out of touch, Despenser was increasingly in bad odor with the court, dating back to 1383 when he had led a failed military crusade into Flanders to beat back the French and to ingratiate himself with Pope Urban VI in Rome. But his botched crusade won him withering condemnation, including an excoriating attack from Wyclif.

Despenser had raised funds for this crusade by taking money from Christians paying for forgiveness to then slaughter Christians. Assisted by his clerk, Henry Bowet, he reimbursed England for the cost of the crusade. Despenser moved to reassert his power with a merciless crackdown on Lollardy. Bishop's Lynn in particular was in his sights, having rioted when he and his men had paraded into town years before.

The cleric who had spied on Sawtrey rushed in and whispered in Despenser's ear, "Sawtrey is inciting heresy in Lynn." The church warhorse stood up and marched out of the room.

The next Sunday, Sawtrey gave a sermon with a message that would deliver a concussive impact felt as far away as Lambeth Palace in London, where the primate of the church, Archbishop Arundel, sat eating his breakfast.

Sawtrey said, his voice slowly rising, "It is wrong to worship relics and images, when our Lord Jesus Christ has given you his living word to live by. Do not worship the wood of the cross, but Christ who suffered upon it. Give your money to the poor. Do not waste it on relics or pilgrimages to the stone-dead monuments of Saints Peter, Paul, or Thomas."

Then Sawtrey really crossed the line, "Do not worship what is material bread, but only seek God in heaven. For even after the consecration of the bread in Eucharist, it still remains material bread." A catalog of Lollard beliefs. These words were Sawtrey's first steps on the road to his execution.

On April 30, 1399, Bishop Despenser hauled Sawtrey in and exhaustively examined him. Sawtrey stuck to his beliefs and was jailed in an episcopal prison, the moldy white stone reeking of urine. A month later, Sawtrey recanted at a public hearing outside St. James's Chapel in Bishop's Lynn before a crowd of townspeople. Bishop Despenser sat in a plush wooden chair brought outside especially for the occasion, his clerics' robes billowing in the morning air. "I reject all of my prior beliefs and statements, and I will never preach them again," Sawtrey said, vowing also to obtain a diocesan license to hear confessions.

Despenser then stood up and loudly announced for all to hear, "Lollardy is an evil perversion, as Fr. Sawtrey just attested. Let him be an example of my forbearance, for he shall be given just a penance." But the next morning, Sawtrey again had to publicly recant before the church at the Hospital of St. John the Baptist in town. John Rickinghall, confessor to the Duke of Bedford, sat listening with Despenser, grim.

Sawtrey moved to London to work as the parish priest of St. Osyth's, Walbrook, just outside the city, putting ample distance between himself and Despenser. But, as agents of Rome hovered, he again preached Lollard beliefs. This time Sawtrey drew the attention of Thomas Arundel, who had only recently regained power as Archbishop of Canterbury in a stunning turn of events.

Years before, King Richard II had banished his cousin, Henry Bolingbroke, and Thomas Arundel as threats to his reign. He had already killed Arundel's brother for treason, and now he stripped Arundel of his office as primate of England, seizing his property.

Richard II had committed acts of tyranny. He had murdered and jailed his enemies, had overtaxed and overspent. The king bought loyalty by confiscating land and castles, giving the property instead to cronies.

Meanwhile, Henry Bolingbroke had won the hearts of the people. With his martial derring-do, Bolingbroke returned along with Arundel from exile and overthrew Richard II, ending 245 years of Plantagenet rule. Arundel was reappointed Archbishop of Canterbury, leader of the church in England, and Bolingbroke was crowned King Henry IV. But King Richard II died in captivity, believed murdered. Some thought he starved to death chewing his own arm. King Henry IV's credibility was deeply, irretrievably damaged. He would face at least ten plots to either overthrow or kill him.

Arundel was autocratic, impatient, and to his backers, diamond-hard brilliant. Always in tune with the winning side, he had the obsessive ability to see around political corners to stop any threat to his authority. But now invisible, darkling forces were creating fault lines in the castle of his religious power. Try as he might, Arundel could not find out who exactly was behind this growing insurgency, ratcheting up his neurotic fear. Everything he had built was now, once again, at risk of being lost for good.

Lollard tracts had been discovered in a growing number of towns, demanding the king seize or tax the church's wealth. Arundel owned a number of manors, the grandest of which, in Holborn, had all the pomp and glitter of court, with a stable of up to eighty horses and a large staff.

As fast as the clergy seized the tracts, a new lot turned up on the street, including copies of the incriminating *Opus Arduum*. This persuasive treatise said the pope was the Antichrist leading the faithful into damnation and that England was in the end times.

The Lollard tracts fueled the growing belief that Arundel was an illegitimate power monger giving religious sanction to the criminal overthrow of a king. Already, a clique of Lollard knights were ensconced at court, gaining the whip hand. King Henry IV was loyal to these devoted soldiers who protected his embattled reign. If it was easy for peasants to try to toss out an established authority during the Peasants' Revolt, it would be even easier to overthrow an illegitimate usurper and his religious accomplice. England was about to be embroiled in civil war once more.

But Arundel and Henry IV would turn around their encroaching feeling of impotency to inflict a ferocious thrashing England had never seen. The country was about to get a bracing dose of authoritarian efficiency in the ugliest of ways.

In the late fall of 1400, Arundel and his lieutenants were in the middle of a fierce debate at Lambeth Palace. One side urged a crackdown on the Lollards, the other, Christian forbearance and the art of persuasion.

The clerics stopped fighting and sat uneasy before a silent Arundel. They studied his face, for Arundel liked to keep them guessing at his blank expression. His glacial countenance projected power and an outsized belief in his moral correctness, which he was about to impose full-bore on England.

"You're trying to impose rules on a mystery that's beyond rules, and that is faith," a divinity student said to a beer keg of a friar.

"But the Lollards are of the utmost—" the friar stammered, searching for the right word, as the divinity student chuckled.

Arundel said through his teeth, "Immature, immoderate. Remember I let you be apprenticed here solely to teach your father childrearing." The student stopped laughing. Arundel turned back.

"Lollards are pretender priests who crush Holy Scriptures through the sieve of the simpleton," the friar, lymphatic, continued. "The more the unlearned teach Jesus's truth, the more our Lord's truth is degraded."

The divinity student butted in again, "But Jesus and his apostles had no university degrees."

Arundel roared, "Silence."

After a moment, he spoke. "England for too long has tolerated lawlessness," he said, his voice sharp with anger, temples throbbing. "This pampering has let all things diabolical take root in the land. It is a wonder God hasn't annihilated us all in one day. Church policy has been passive and ad hoc for too long. It has opened the door to Satan and his will to power. Satan divides us to rule us."

Arundel turned to look at a senior monk he respected who was quietly listening. Days before, the monk had prayed with Arundel against the temptations of power, about how men made whole by power were hollowed out by it, too.

Finally the monk spoke, "Your grace, pry loose the claws of vengeance from your heart. You will cripple your immortal soul. The devil is devious, he holds us spellbound, that all that matters is power. Let us not react like Pharisees bent on absolute power. Forgiveness is what our Savior taught. The Lollards do not attack the faith. They attack men corrupting the faith. Focus on the fallen and redeem the church in England."

But Arundel frowned back at him. His word was usually absolute, he liked being dry-eyed and even keeled, strong of will. Now he wasn't. This was a strange feeling. He didn't like it.

The friar turned on the senior monk, "You speak with such cock-sureness as if you yourself have held office since Henry II. You cannot appease an evil that bashes down our doors to steal from our charities. Change will come with lightning speed and violence in uprisings worse than the one that took our Sudbury."

The divinity student meekly pointed out, "Perhaps all we need to do is arrest the writer of the *Opus Arduum*. A jailer found words like this tract scribbled on a prison wall. Capture that heretic."

The friar sullenly agreed, "That is the way. Find the cankered soul at the root. Nicholas Hereford perhaps wrote it. He was arrested. He preached disendowment at St. Frideswide's. Good God, that was already twenty years ago. And he is from that Lollard lunatic Oldcastle's hometown. Lollard knights imprisoned him."

But the senior monk disagreed, "No, the *Arduum* writer said the bishops were his jailers, not the knights, so it couldn't have been Hereford."

The friar offered, "Perhaps John Purvey, Wyclif's fellow, wrote it. He had the gall to argue the king could even depose a pope."

Again the senior monk interjected, "There is no one head of Lollardy. And why are we so concerned? We can just show the people that the Lollards are the same bunch of deranged conspiracy mongers like Valentinus obsessing about whatever secret code they think they see in the Bible. Every century has men who think they and only they know the secrets in scriptures to a better world to come."

But Arundel was on a different track. He leaned back, fingertips making a tent in front of his face, "The writer of the *Arduum* is clearly university-trained. He's intelligent enough to link the persecution of his fellow schismatics with the burning of manuscripts written by friars Peter John Olivi and John of Rupescissa. The problem is

Oxford University. That pile of ragwort has been suffocating the good grain of Christ's word for years."

At that point, another friar entered the meeting room and interrupted the debate. "Here's more, your grace," he announced as he led a group of men who dumped confiscated booklets on the table.

"'England only owes obedience to the king and nothing to the church,'" the friar read aloud. "'Arundel is Caesar resurrected.' The same words, over and over."

Arundel hissed, "Exterminate these schism fomenters, these sons of anger and discord."

The senior monk replied, flabbergasted, "But your grace, we'll never stop them because there is no one, main source. There are thousands of them now. It is better to forgive. The church has been here before. Lollards are merely the same old original sin of Adam."

But the friar blew up, "Precisely why we must fight them. Prideful, ignorant pharaohs who believe their imagination divine. Grasp the nettle. The Lollards poison innocents in our care by the thousands every day, damning them to hell."

Nothing energized Arundel more than hypocrisy, because it touched a self-recognition deep down inside that he had done all he could to drum it out of his soul. Yes, he and Henry had won under dubious circumstances, but what was that compared to the injustices and crimes daily meted out by Richard's court? Arundel interrupted, "The heroes of their own stories. The serendipity of stumbling on ideas in the Bible to justify their self-interest."

The friar nodded, "England will soon find a Lollard as pope of their own church. We must lead them back to the common good. Our capacity for moral humility, for trusting in divine grace, makes the New Jerusalem possible. But it is man's capacity for self-love and pride—Babylon—that makes us necessary."

Arundel stood up, slammed his fists on the table, and roared, "Wipe these children of the devil off the face of the earth."

The divinity student said timidly, "But your grace, we have no power to ask the crown to do that. And the Lollards are very large in number, the people respect them."

Again Arundel smacked his hand on the table and said, "Go to my steward outside and have him lock you in your room, you reliable font of excretia."

As the student walked out, the gathering fell into scared silence. Arundel sneered, "How quaint, how irrelevant we've become. We sit here like dithering milkmaids while right in our midst a hydra of talking heads is condemning innocent souls to eternal damnation. We sit here trying to name our enemies, not seeing that they are not known to us because they are not countries flying standards. They are blank faces operating in the shadows. How safe do any of you feel knowing your baker, your tailor, your butcher hates you and seeks your destruction?"

Alarmed at his rage, the senior monk said, "Perhaps that is the answer, your grace. We can show the people that Lollards are prideful hypocrites. But do not yourself fall prey to pride."

Arundel snarled with unconcealed hostility, "You are a reed, not an oak. Kindness weakens."

He turned back to the gathering and continued, cold as ice, "The thrust and cut of this debate bores me. I live in a kingdom of nitwits, surrounded by sniping mediocrity. By men unburdened of intellect. All of you are no more fit than a donkey playing a gittern."

As they sat back, Arundel continued, "The Lollards have no idea the powers they face. There is an ulterior motive here. Sedition. Treason. We can convince the king that Lollards are committing crimes against the state, creating their own country of the saved, separating Christians from Christians, Christians from church, Christians from kingdom."

Arundel paused for a moment and thought. Then, like a burst of fiery sunlight, the answer dawned on him, the perfect answer to convince a king who loved his Gospel more than anything.

"Open your Bibles to Matthew 13:24–30," Arundel ordered.

"The parable of the good seed?" asked the friar.

"My groom cannot think as slow as you even if he tried," Arundel steamed. "Read."

The cleric read aloud Jesus's parable as Arundel sat back, "The kingdom of heaven is like a man who sowed good seed in the field, where his enemy came and sowed weeds. I will tell the harvesters, 'First collect the weeds and tie them in bundles to be burned. Then gather the wheat and bring it into my barn.'"

Arundel raised his hand and they all fell silent, as he waited smiling, watching. The clerics look at each other, baffled.

But it suddenly dawned fully on the divinity student eavesdropping outside. "The word Lollard is derived from the Latin word *lollium*, which means a useless weed," he said in shock to the clerics as Arundel's happy visage chilled the marrow of their bones to ice. The leader of the church in England then stood up, put his knuckles on the table, and leaned forward.

"'Come to choke out the good seed, the children of God,'" Arundel finished the Gospel quote. "Burn them."

CHAPTER TWELVE

• • •

First Burned

The most terrifying piece of legislation England had ever seen was about to become the law of the land in 1401.

For the first time, the country enacted a death penalty for heresy, which Arundel championed and Henry IV backed, sealing his fate as the first king of England to legalize the burning of his countrymen for differences of religious opinion. Even though the new law didn't exactly define what heresy was, church and state were so gung ho about it, they defined the law on the fly, with a vengeance.

Heretics had been burnt alive in Ireland or on the continent, but not in England. Now the new law, *De Haeretico Comburendo*, let the church in England convict people of heresy in its own courts, handing over those who refused to recant to then be burnt to death by the court. Arundel would later back another law, the *Constitutions*, which censored all teachings contradicting the tenets of the faith, "rooting out the evil weeds" of heresy. It also outlawed buying, reading or manufacturing any unapproved translation of the Bible in English, including the Wyclif Bible, and unauthorized, freelance preaching without a diocesan license.

A cleric raced in to Archbishop Arundel's chambers and said, "Your grace, have you heard William Sawtrey of Bishop's Lynn moved here to London after recanting, just so he could preach heresies again?" Arundel quickly had Sawtrey arrested and ordered to stand trial.

On Saturday, February 12, 1401, Sawtrey was marched into the chapter house of the imposing St. Paul's Cathedral, where the greatest powers of England's church were assembled. Arundel sat in the middle of a tribunal of archbishops, bishops, and clergymen, soft, uncalloused hands folded in their laps, ready to examine Lynn's prodigal son, about to become Arundel's greatest atrocity.

Sawtrey unfolded a scroll and bravely read aloud, "I, William Sawtrey, priest unworthy, say and answer that I will not nor intend to worship the wood of the cross upon which Christ was crucified. I will only worship Christ who suffered upon the cross. Yet, notwithstanding, I will worship the cross as a memorial of the passion of Christ."

Hearing equivocation, Arundel and his panel pounded Sawtrey for several days about his beliefs, focusing on transubstantiation. Exhausted, but still sticking to his sense of integrity, Sawtrey finally admitted, "I cannot tell if the bread becomes Jesus."

Seeing insolence, the archbishop sat up and shouted, "Will you submit to the authority of the church on this matter?"

Sawtrey replied, "If it is not contrary to the will of God." After more hours of questioning, Sawtrey finally undercut himself, "The host remains just material bread, even after the words of the sacrament are spoken."

To prove he relapsed again, Arundel submitted Bishop Despenser's trial records of Sawtrey, covering his role in the affair. When shown his prior recantation, Sawtrey admitted to teaching Lollardy again. He was then sentenced to be spiritually and emotionally destroyed by the ritual humiliation of a public demotion at St. Paul's Cathedral.

On February 26, 1401, clerics stepped forward in gleaming black robes belted by narrow violet cords. They murmured ancient Latin texts as they summarily stripped Sawtrey of his pastoral authority in seven successive stages. Sawtrey was ordered to hold up and then have removed his paten, chalice, his copy of the Bible, and his keys to the church. They put on and then pulled from his back the robes of each order: priest, deacon, subdeacon, acolyte, exorcist, reader, and finally, church doorkeeper. Novice clerics fought back tears as they sat Sawtrey down to shave off his tonsure. Sawtrey looked in their eyes and whispered, "I've already forgiven you."

After they stuck a demeaning, green wool cap on his head like a yeoman, Sawtrey, still not comprehending the danger he was in, boldly said to Arundel sitting in the middle of the panel, "Your malice against me was already consummated before this trial. What more evil can you do to me?"

Arundel gave him a withering stare and looked at the tribunal. "The debauched clown has revealed his true nature, pride," the archbishop said. Then he looked back to Sawtrey, paused, and stood up.

Unbeknownst to Sawtrey, the archbishop had already been in close contact with the king and Parliament, laying the groundwork for the death penalty. So powerful was Arundel, and so angry had this little pastor of Bishop's Lynn made him, that Sawtrey was condemned to death even before the new death penalty officially became law.

"Rise, Sawtrey," Arundel commanded, as a petrifying silence deadened the church. "We degrade and depose you before the high constable and marshal of England. You are excommunicated, cast out."

Arundel then read aloud the king's order to the marshal sitting there, "As far as it is in us to pluck up the roots of heresies, I do command you to commit William to the fire, to be burned in a public, open place for detestation of his crime."

They then shoved Sawtrey out of the church and into the arms of the secular authorities. As he walked in chains outside, the crowd grew enraged. "What kind of church kills its own priest?" came the shouts, increasing in fury as the bishops walked out.

A baker bellowed at Arundel, "You are worse than Caesar, worse than Judas. You have condemned yourself to hell."

Still another heckler yelled, "We are blind sheep led by blind wolves. Archbishop Arundel, when were you and your Sanhedrin exempted from the Ten Commandments?"

Morning dawned grey a few days later on March 2. The jailers smacked their keys against Sawtrey's prison door to wake him up. "Stand up," they ordered. Sawtrey ignored them and continued to kneel, deep in prayer, as they stripped him and threw a hemp robe over his head. They locked Sawtrey in chains, picked him up, and placed him on a hurdle, a piece of movable fence, which they then used to drag him on to Smithfield.

Smithfield sat just northwest of London's city walls, a place of increasing bleakness, where the Scottish rebel, William Wallace, was executed a century prior and where a plague pit for victims of the Black Death was dug.

The procession stopped before the scaffolding as one of the executioners decided to take a drink. Fighting back tears, Sawtrey turned to the crowd and said, "I pray for my king and my bishop. I pray for God's love and mercy. In minutes I will be tied to the wood of an elm tree, the arms of its branches my last home on earth. But just as this elm tree came from the seeds of love's creation, let love be the seed of our forgiveness."

Men and women broke down crying as the executioners shoved Sawtrey back down on the hurdle, but the crowd burst through and hugged him one last time in a desperate clutch. Sawtrey whispered, "Pray for me that I will be brought home to the great love waiting for all of us at the quiet borders of the earth. Pray for me, as I will for you when I walk into the New Jerusalem."

The crowd grabbed at his tunic while Sawtrey was pulled away. They placed Sawtrey atop a huge pile of branches and locked his wrists behind him in chains at a wooden stake, facing out. An open-ended barrel was then placed over his head, thought to be a humanitarian move as it would create a funnel of immediate death. Then, before an enormous crowd of onlookers, his executioners lit the fire and burned him, the first martyr of the Reformation.

Sawtrey screamed in agony and shock, realizing he had no idea how painful this death would be. Choked with blue-black smoke, he couldn't catch his breath to cry out in pain. He threw up a shot of bile through the tower of flames.

The men and women present there were initially excited with their communal solidarity over the coming spectacle. But then they watched the chains locking his wrists burn away from the stake, letting Sawtrey put his face in his hands behind the flames. They recognized the same familiar gesture he made when praying in church. The crowd reeled back in horror, many vomiting, as they watched a devouring wall of fire overtake Sawtrey, the flames turning the seconds into hours, the archangels' hands reaching.

Back in Bishop's Lynn, the people were gripped by a nauseating, emotional fear that their world was changing and that they couldn't do anything about it. Margery, John, and their friends stood aghast with the rest of the townspeople in the village square as the town crier read aloud a statement from the church, "Sawtrey has been burnt for his wicked beliefs. Under penalty of law, you must no longer speak of him."

As her husband, Thomas, and William stood glumly looking down at the floor, Catherine cried out in anguish in her kitchen upon hearing the news, "How is burning a Catholic priest saving the life of the church?"

Outraged that they had no answer, she shouted at them, "You and William spent your day at a place of horror, why?"

Thomas said, crying, "To support him, Catherine." But he and William couldn't speak because they still had the rank smell of the scorched priest in their nostrils. They stood in tears knowing this memory would cling to them until the day they died. Catherine finally said, "We are now led by ignorant, common murderers. The cruelest storm has now set upon us from within. It will take the measure of us all."

William finally said, "All the fire in England could never touch Sawtrey's soul."

Meanwhile, Archbishop Arundel's men were reassuring him as he sat doused in guilt in his chambers at Lambeth Palace. "It has only just begun," he finally said.

His aide replied, "Not so. This is an act of mercy. Eternal damnation is worse than the few moments of pain at a predestinate stake they deserve. The people will see. And Sawtrey will soon be forgotten because the men of tomorrow are just as self-interested as the men of today."

Despite Sawtrey's gruesome death, the Lollards kept coming. After four years, the prisons started to fill to capacity with accused heretics and seditionists, including priests, the church executing a number of them, letting many go with a penance. The kingdom still insolvent, the Commons again took up the Lollards' call to seize or tax church property in 1404 and 1406. By then Henry IV was deathly ill, and was handing over power to a royal council to rule. Even though he was reappointed Lord Chancellor in January 1407, a position he held in 1389, Arundel fought these moves by himself, isolated and alone.

Henry IV died on March 20, 1413, just shy of his forty-sixth birthday. The bottom half of his body was said to have shriveled. Arundel died in February 1414, complaining his throat was being attacked. But the persecution of the Lollards continued. Meanwhile, Margery and John Kempe's problems were just beginning.

. . .

CHAPTER THIRTEEN

Chastity in Marriage

*M*argery and John continued in their uneasy marriage. One day, in a state of extreme agitation, she paced from kitchen to backyard to kitchen, red-faced and disheveled. She was trying to become a chaste, secular vowess who, unlike a nun, would live in the world so as to stay with her family.

"I beg you John, please now take a vow of chastity so as to avoid divine displeasure over our sinful ways of the flesh," Margery demanded.

Outwardly he remained calm, but inside John was confused. His wife was now saying he faced supernatural wrath for something he felt was as natural as breathing. He especially loved to hold Margery on bitter cold, winter nights. "It's so cold I saw the pardoner finally put his hands in his pockets," he remembered Thomas joking to him the other day.

John looked out the window and thought, grimacing, "So now we are to live as widower and widow." Curt as a farmer, he could only reply, "Maybe." John watched for her reaction from his peripheral vision. His marriage was dying, his wife was becoming reborn in Christ, and there was nothing he could do about it.

Running a big household wasn't easy. The Kempes had run up a massive debt, and they were trying to apprentice out the older children to learn trades in the homes of nobles and merchants. "I am not ready for this atoning sacrifice," John thought. "I do not want to live together alone. Marital love is not evil."

But Margery was still talking, "Jesus has also commanded me to make a pilgrimage to Jerusalem."

This new demand was highly dangerous, a grueling voyage of two thousand miles over treacherous land and seas. Still, a pilgrimage to the Holy Land was the pinnacle of Christian life. It would deliver forgiveness of all sins, grant immediate entry into heaven, and improve a Christian's reputation damaged by gossips in town. Also, upon returning, pilgrims would be asked to pray for sick people and the deceased, their prayers famously powerful for wiping out years in purgatory.

A wife needed her husband's permission to go, however, and John would not give it. "You could be raped or robbed on pilgrimage," John finally said. "You know as well as I your father has warned everyone that cutthroats like the Folville and Coterel gangs still escape the town watch and claim sanctuary. What am I to do, trust you to just the weather and the heathland roads?"

John knelt beside her and spoke softly, "Margery, don't you see? Even just walking down the road, you could die, just like that glove merchant who fell and drowned in that clay pit near Aylesbury."

But Margery looked down, not speaking. They went to bed upset that night. The next morning Margery offered a bright compromise, "John, let's you and I go on pilgrimage here, for our spiritual and physical health." John smiled. Domestic pilgrimages were more doable, safer, and cheaper. There was plenty to see, like the coals used to roast St. Lawrence, St. Edmund's fingernails, and an image of St. Modwen with her red cow and staff that pregnant women prayed to.

After they arranged for Eleanor and William to watch the children, the Kempes started on a brisk country walk through the

English countryside to York, a city home to numerous churches and religious houses, like the Minster.

Once there, they went to the shrine of the head of St. Hugh of Lincoln, a famous Carthusian bishop who had died in 1200. St. Hugh had refurbished a monastery for poor monks and had tried to protect local Jews from vicious attacks. They watched a white swan walk by, as a monk said, "That is the offspring of St. Hugh's companion. It guarded him while he slept. A swan now visits his grave." An elderly priest shuffled out of the back with a parcel wrapped in old, decayed brown linens. The Kempes said an Our Father over the relic of St. Hugh's head.

At a local church, Margery loudly sobbed, impressing and offending visitors gathered there. "What is wrong with her?" a local asked another, who couldn't say.

John and Margery then went to an alehouse for dinner. A summer hot spell was upon them, long nights filled with heat lightning. Having gone without sex for two months, John wanted to make love to his wife, but he was unsure. As they sat at the table drinking ale, John asked, "Do you Margery—do you still love me? Lie with me tonight."

She vehemently shook her head no, then launched into a homiletic, "We will find God in chastity."

John watched Margery talking, her voice fading away, only lips moving to mouth words building a fieldstone wall around her heart. His entire marriage was now distilled into this very moment, and he didn't know what to do. They went to bed, the darkness heavy, humid.

The next morning, a light, predawn rain through the open window of the inn awakened John. Still frustrated, after breakfast he took Margery arm in arm. They continued to walk under a hot, midsummer sun, swatting away at clouds of midges. After a few miles, they sat down by the side of the road, a highway cross nearby in a field.

John said, "Margery, resubmit and resume your marital vows." But Margery remained silent. "Where is my wife?" John wondered. He tried a different tack.

John asked, "Margery, if there came a man with a sword who would strike off my head unless I made love with you as I used to do before, tell me on your conscience—for you say you will not lie—whether you would allow my head to be cut off, or else allow me to make love with you again?"

Exasperated, Margery said, "Sir, why are you raising this matter when we have been chaste for these past eight weeks?"

John answered quietly, "Because I want to know the truth of your heart," even though he feared what she had to say.

Margery grew profoundly sad. She couldn't lie. "Alas, I would rather see you being killed than that we should turn back to our uncleanness," she finally answered, looking down.

John was stunned, and blushed deeply. Then he grew angry. Yes, his marriage had its share of marathon sulks and stormy silences, but nothing so damaging as this. "You are no good wife," he finally said.

But Margery turned the tables on him. "Then what was the reason that you have not made love to me these last eight weeks?" she asked.

"I was made afraid to do so by you. I dared not touch you," John replied.

That was an opening. John was admitting sex was wrong. Margery stood up and said, "Now, good sir, mend your ways and ask God's mercy, for I told you nearly three years ago that our desire for sex would suddenly be slain."

As John stared at the ground, Margery said more gently, "Good sir, I pray you to grant what I shall ask, and I shall pray for you to be saved through the mercy of our Lord Jesus Christ."

Margery then knelt on the ground before him and grasped his hands in hers. "And you shall have more reward in heaven than if you wore a hair shirt or a coat of mail as a penance," she said, looking for his eyes. "I pray you, allow me to make a vow of chastity at whichever bishop's hand that God wills."

But then John realized he could be damned to hell if he had sex with her after they took a vow of chastity. He said flatly, "No, I won't allow you to do that, because now I can make love to you without mortal sin and then I wouldn't be able to."

But Margery was not backing down. She stood up and said, "If it be the will of the Holy Ghost to fulfill what I have said, I pray God you may consent to this." However, she still tried to reason with him and said, half-joking, "And if it be not the will of the Holy Ghost, I pray God that you never consent."

But that only left John even more confused. The two continued walking toward Bridlington in the north, the sun still beating down. There they planned to see the shrine of St. John of Bridlington, who had died about two decades earlier and was only recently canonized. King Henry V later attributed his astounding victory over a much larger French force at the Battle of Agincourt to St. John's intercession (and his eagle-eyed archers).

Another highway cross loomed in the distance. Walking up to it, John sat under it, despondent, conflicted. At the time, husbands were legally allowed to beat their disobedient wives into submission, so long as they didn't physically damage them. In fact, a man had so brutally beaten his wife a few years back, he had knocked her teeth out and had left her mentally disabled. But that was not John's nature. Wives, in turn, could take their husbands to court and charge them with cruelty, even though they must still be sexually faithful to abusive husbands according to their marriage vows—with many prayers offered to St. Wyglefort, the patron saint of abused wives.

Tired of fighting, John finally said, "Margery, grant me my desire and I shall grant you your desire."

Margery perked up. "What is it?" she asked.

"My first desire is that we shall still lie together in one bed as we have done before," John said. "The second, that you shall pay my debts before you go to Jerusalem. And the third, that you shall eat and drink with me on Fridays as you used to, and stop fasting."

He added, "Fridays is when we make merry, you and I. It is our routine. Then, and only then, will I let you go on pilgrimage."

But while fasting was meaningless to John, and Christians were already required to fast more than two months out of the year, to Margery, fasting was much more. "No, sir," Margery replied adamantly. "I will never agree to break my Friday fast as long as I live."

John said angrily, "Well then, I'm going to have sex with you again," moving toward her. But Margery startled him. She fell to her knees, desperate. "I beg you John. Give me leave to make my prayers," she gasped.

Audibly weeping, her back to John, Margery knelt before the wayside cross and prayed loudly, "You know what sorrow I have had to be chaste for you in my body all these three years, and now I might have my will and I dare not, for love of you." Then she added, "Now, blessed Jesus, make your will known to my unworthy self, so that I may afterwards follow your will and fulfill it with all my might."

Jesus gave her the answer. Margery relayed it to John, "Grant me that you will not come into my bed, and I grant you that I will pay your debts before I go to Jerusalem. And make my body free to God, so that you never make any claim on me requesting any conjugal debt after this day as long as you live. And I shall eat and drink on Fridays at your bidding."

John finally gave in. "May your body be as freely available to God as it has been to me," he said. Margery hugged him and replied, "I thank God greatly. We must pray three Paternosters in worship of the Holy Trinity before the cross."

When they finished praying, Margery and John stood up from kneeling and sat down off to the side of the cross. She uncorked a bottle of ale, as her husband took out a cake tucked inside his shirt. All was good, Margery thought.

The whole affair, though, left John deeply sad. He looked silently into the bottle, his eyes stinging. That night, Margery snored quietly as they slept in a small barn. But John was awake, hardly sleeping into the small hours.

The next day they didn't speak for a while as they walked to Bridlington, the spoor of animals underfoot in the dark, musty woods. Once in Bridlington, John stood by as his wife shopped at a goldsmith in town, buying a new gold ring engraved inside with the words *Jesus est amor meus*, "Jesus is my love." She would wear it just as nuns do to show they are brides of Christ. But soon, things again took a turn for the worse.

CHAPTER FOURTEEN

• • •

Canterbury Monks

*M*argery and John then went to Canterbury Cathedral to visit England's most popular pilgrim site, the tomb of St. Thomas Becket, martyred by followers of King Henry II. Renowned as a shrine for healing, the Kempes looked at the little wax models of feet, legs, arms, hands, heads, farm animals, and ships other pilgrims had left as requests for help. Offerings of oatcakes, cheese, wool, and cups with herbs sat nearby.

Canterbury was avowedly anti-Lollard. A priest was riling the local clergy in town, "You must stop the scattering of the Gospel by the ignorant who are so presumptuous as to dispute clerics in public." Reginald Pecock, bishop of nearby Chicester, was also warning about "arrogant women Lollards speaking haughtily about clerics." Meanwhile, Margery heard Jesus telling her, "Don't be afraid. Those that hear you hear the voice of God."

At Mass at Christ Church in Canterbury, Margery repeatedly fell on the ground, sobbing, "I die. I die for love of you, Jesus." Her outburst triggered a wave of alarm that rolled through pew after pew. Initial compassion soon curdled into resentment.

"The devil himself has turned her into a half-wit chatterbox, a self-important fake," said a local parishioner after Mass.

"Surely she is some kind of heretic. She should be arrested," replied an older woman.

A senior monk overheard them and said to a novice, "Lollard activity in East Anglia where this woman is from is fervent." They hurried away to warn a powerful church official.

Generally ruthless, John Kynton had quit his post as treasurer to the glittering Queen Joanna Navarre, wife of King Henry IV, to enter the religious life. He was exactly the mixture of secular official-priest Wyclif and the Lollards detested. Kynton looked up expectantly, "Yes, what now?"

"A false woman from Bishop's Lynn is teaching scripture, forbidden by law," the younger monk said.

"Perhaps she just gossips like a jackdaw," replied Kynton, turning back to his work.

The senior monk said loudly, "Forbidden by God's law. St. Paul's first letter to Timothy, chapter two, verse twelve."

Kynton stared him into submission, "Quote St. Bernard." When the monk couldn't, he said tartly, "Eve spoke but once and threw the whole world into disorder."

The senior monk then bowed deeply, and said, "Your grace, a married mother of fourteen children dressed all in white is walking around in public preaching, just like the vagabond nuns of Polsloe. But she refuses to prostrate herself as a nun. These pretenders are turning the Christian world shambolic. She will corrupt parishioners, especially our wives." But he was talking to an empty room, because Kynton had already left to hunt down Margery.

Meanwhile, John Kempe had walked out of Christ Church and left behind his boisterous wife as if she was a stranger, startled at the people's reaction to her, still upset they had grown apart. Margery watched him go. She finally walked out, right into the path of Kynton. "Come sit with me. Let's talk in the garden out back," he said, as the senior monk with the novice arrived.

As they all sat down, Kynton asked, "What can you say of God?"

Margery replied, "Sir, I will both speak of him and hear of him."
With an almost perfect memory, she then recounted nearly verbatim
a story from the Bible. But reciting Scripture was against the law.
Irked, Kynton scolded, "I wish you were enclosed in a house of stone,
so that no one should speak with you."

But instead of taking it quietly, Margery poked him in the eye,
"Ah, sir, you should support God's servants, and you are the first that
holds against them, our Lord amend you."

As Kynton fumed watching Margery walk away toward the town
gate, the senior monk vehemently whispered in his ear, "Women
banded together for the uplift of humanity can be just as intolerant
as the busy bee Pharisees. Never cease to excoriate the sin of pride
in the form of *libido sciendi*. You see here her insolent lust to know
and teach the Bible, just like a Lollard. As well as the signal vice of
women, gabbling."

Marching after Margery, the novice monk overtook her and said,
"Either you have the Holy Ghost or else you have a devil within you,
for what you are speaking here to us is Holy Writ and that you do
not have of yourself."

Meanwhile, a crowd was gathering just outside the gate, a growing
danger. The curfew bell would ring in just a few hours, which meant
the gate would be closed. Margery would have to sleep alone on the
streets if she didn't find shelter. Seeing she was surrounded, Margery
decided to save herself with a story. She stepped up on a small boulder
and said, "Give me leave to tell you a tale." The crowd shouted, "Let
her say what she wants."

Margery spoke forcefully. "There was once a man who had sinned
greatly against God, and when he was shriven, his confessor enjoined
him as part of his penance that he should for one year hire men to
chide him and reprove him for his sins, and he should give them silver
for their labor. And one day he came amongst many great men, such

as are here now, God save you all, and stood among them as I now stand amongst you, they despising him as you do me, the man all the while laughing and smiling and having good sport at their words."

Margery continued, "The chief among them said to the man, 'Why are you laughing, you wretch, when you are being greatly despised?' And he answered, 'I have great cause to laugh, because now I don't have to pay any money to take my sin of pride away from me.'"

A man in the crowd said, "Aha, so he didn't have to pay to be chastised because they were doing it for free."

Margery nodded, teaching them a lesson about her vocation. "Right so I say to you, while I was at home in my own part of the country, day by day with great weeping and mourning I sorrowed because I did not have any of the shame, scorn, and contempt that I deserved. I thank you all highly, sirs, for what, morning and afternoon, I have received today in rightful measure, blessed be God for it."

Tricked, humiliated, the Canterbury monks looked at each other, scrambling to find a scriptural twig to pull themselves out of the torrent of recriminating looks from the crowd.

"Clearly, this insolent women just indicted herself by trying to assert her right to speak, tell her that," the senior monk hissed as he shoved the younger monk forward, now looking around warily.

"You take her on. You yourself heard this moralizing upstart of a woman with no more wit than a goose claiming direct access to Jesus, defying us," he whispered back.

"Heretic," the Canterbury monks started off slowly shouting at her back as Margery walked toward the gate, oblivious to the mayhem in her wake.

Then it got worse. Branches stuck in a barrel sat in a cart nearby, the monks agreed they could use it to take Margery to the stake. "You shall be burnt, you false Lollard," they railed. "Here is a cart full of thorns ready for you and a barrel to burn you with."

Now scared and alone, Margery whirled around in circles. She watched as even more people came looking for entertainment, the setting sun turning their faces black. The crowd's appetite increased. "Take her and burn her," the people jeered, tightening the circle around her.

Paralyzed by fear, Margery stood stock still, her heart beating like a trip-hammer. She desperately scanned the crowd searching for her husband. Then Margery looked up to the sky and prayed, tears welling, "I came to this place, Lord, for love of you. Help me and have mercy on me." But Jesus didn't answer.

Seeing her distress, two handsome young students pushed through the crowd and stood in front of Margery. They loudly asked for all to hear, "Are you neither a heretic nor a Lollard?"

"No, sirs. I am neither heretic nor Lollard," Margery beamed gratefully.

The young students turned back around, protecting her, chins out. Slowly, grudgingly, one by one the crowd dispersed. After all were gone, one of the young men asked Margery, "Where are you staying?"

Margery replied, "I don't remember. I think the inn is run by a German."

Remembering priests robed in scarlet at one of the local inns, the two took her to her lodgings. In the three walked, and there Margery found her husband John. Setting aside her confusion about him, she relayed her near-death experience. Worried, the couple decided to hurry back to Bishop's Lynn in the morning.

CHAPTER FIFTEEN

Patron Saint of Gossip

*O*n the way home to Bishop's Lynn, John stared stoically ahead, trying to make it home safely. Margery softly cried as she thought ruefully about the confrontation. Her thoughts turned morbid.

Perhaps already tired of the mockery and rejection, Margery daydreamed about the martyrdom she might die for Jesus, of drowning in the ocean or being blown away by a hurricane, or having her head chopped off with a sharp axe, an easy death compared to burning.

But Christ suddenly appeared in her mind's eye. "I thank you, daughter, that you would be willing to suffer death for my love. You shall have the same reward in heaven as if you had suffered that same death," Jesus told her. "Yet no man shall slay you, nor fire burn you, nor water drown you, nor winds harm you."

Instead, Jesus warned Margery of a martyrdom of a different sort, with no end in death. He had given hints before of her destiny, of the hair shirt in her heart, which had left her anxious. Now Jesus finally cleared up the confusion.

Margery was to become the patron saint of gossip. Whether by her own doing or not, she would be subject to lacerating, backbiting slander, impugned by urbane derision, made a laughingstock in her hometown she loved dearly, and in villages and cities. This way forward was a severely painful road.

Margery would be smeared with all sorts of charges, of lying, hypocrisy, heresy, attacked for trying to stop liars, those who curse, for rebuking the vain and the pompous. "You should have no other purgatory than in this world alone. You shall be crucified daily for your crying," Jesus warned. "You shall be eaten and gnawed by the people of the world just as any rat gnaws the stockfish," just like the rats having at the dried fish out back in the stalls at home.

Margery also would be scorned for seeming to turn on and off her tears at will like a water tap. "Tears of compassion are the highest gift I can give on earth," Jesus said.

"I give you great cries," he added, "in token that I wish that my mother's sorrow be known through you, so that men and women might have more compassion for her sorrow that she suffered for me. I have ordained you to be a mirror amongst them," to show people how to grieve for their sins and be saved.

But then Jesus warned, "You should have no vainglory and should recognize that you may not have tears or spiritual conversing except when God will send them to you. Suffer patiently when I withdraw them."

As John again looked on in wonder at his wife crying, Jesus comforted her, "For the more shame and more contempt that you endure for my love, the more joy shall you have with me in heaven. He that dreads the shame of the world may not perfectly love God."

Moreover, to thwart her attackers, Jesus told Margery, "I shall give you grace enough to answer every cleric in the love of God, so that no devil in hell nor man on earth can take you away from me."

Margery wiped away tears and looked up into the sky as Jesus said he would always be there for her, hidden in the bright uplands she couldn't see.

Jesus said, "Sometimes, the sun shines so that many people can see it and sometimes it is hidden behind a cloud so that it cannot be seen, and yet, it is the sun, nevertheless." He added, "And just so I proceed with you and with my chosen souls. As sure as you are of the sun, when you see it shining brightly, just as sure are you of the love of God. My merciful eyes are ever upon you. It would be impossible for you to suffer the scorns and contempt that you will have were it not for my grace supporting you."

Heartened, Margery stared up at the piercing blue summer sky. She then noticed cumulus clouds gathering, their grey backs towering over the couple down below. Margery squinted to the left of them, the audience of clouds leaning forward, looking ahead, their faces lit blindingly white.

"I take no notice of what a man has been, but I take heed of what he will be," Jesus had told her. A passage from the *Cloud of Unknowing* came to mind. "God looks at what you would become," Margery thought, "And I would, Lord, for your love, be laid naked on a hurdle for all men to wonder at me for your love, so long as it were no danger to their souls, and they to throw mud and slime at me, and to be drawn from town to town and have men throw gobs of mud at me every day of my life, if you were pleased by this."

As he walked, John examined the white beam aspen and pine trees on the sides of the road, while Margery followed the shadows of billowing clouds gently moving over the face of the world, drifting over clutches of flowers, guiding them along.

Once back home, Margery busied herself getting ready for her pilgrimage. But John remained skeptical, more so because of yet another command from God, one that would put his wife in mortal danger.

This vision said that Margery must set aside the uniform of a pilgrim, the grey, bell-sleeved cassock with red crosses stitched on it, as well as the wide-brimmed hat adorned with scallop shell patches. Jesus ordered, "I want you to wear clothes of white and no other color."

That was a dangerous move. Margery was about to set herself at a right angle to church and society, clothed in white like a novice nun, one who didn't renounce the world, but instead chose to live in it. White symbolized purity, virgin undefiled, the holiest of people. White was not meant for English mothers of fourteen children whose husbands were still very much alive.

Her white clothes set the gossips' tongues ululating that Margery was a hypocrite, a claim that was always the first foot in the door toward full-blown charges of heresy. The rich vein of gossip about her had already started to flow through the stalls at the Saturday and Tuesday markets.

Deeply anxious, Margery prayed, "I fear people will slander me." But Jesus reminded her, "Daughter, the more ridicule that you have for love of me, the more you please me." So Margery had no choice. She would publicly cry wearing white. The backlash would be brutal and severe, moreover, the timing couldn't be worse.

Sure enough, the townspeople savaged her. "False hypocrite, deceiver. She is not of God. She is an act of will," Ruth taunted.

Guy piled on, "Her visions are not from God. They are evil spirits parading as angels of light. Now she wants to look like one."

But her husband John defended his wife. "Leave her be. She is of God," he retorted.

Margery consoled him back home, "It is my purgatory on earth to suffer shame and abuse for wearing white."

There was still plenty to do before setting off for Jerusalem and Rome. Margery needed to take a vow of chastity in front of a church official and get his blessing on her pilgrimage, her white clothes, and her new wedding ring to Christ. She also needed references to travel alone to the Holy Land.

Margery arranged to meet with the erudite Bishop of Lincoln, Philip Repingdon. A devoted follower of Wyclif while at the

University of Oxford decades before, Repingdon later recanted after he was charged with heresy in 1382. He then became confessor to King Henry IV, and the king even gave Repingdon his ring after his victory at the Battle of Shrewsbury. Repingdon also traveled with the king in 1406 so the king could kiss the relics in Bardney Abbey in a vain attempt to cure his skin disease.

King Henry V had been crowned about four months prior to the time the Kempes visited Repingdon in the summer of 1413. The new king had captured the country's imagination, a rara avis under an unseen star. He detested Lollards, who had grown even more defiant. Henry V needed calm in the land as he was about to launch yet another campaign to conquer France. Ridding the countryside of troublemakers was key. The court issued royal mandates to ardently stop all signs of heresy.

The Kempes met with Repingdon at his episcopal castle at Sleaford in Lincolnshire. Margery got right to the point about her white clothes, "I am commanded in my soul that you shall give me the mantle and ring." Seeing his reluctance, she reassured him, "If you clothe me on earth, our Lord Jesus Christ shall clothe you in heaven, as I understand through revelation." This last sentence no one could ignore. The bishop sat back in his chair. He turned to John.

"John, is it your will that your wife take the mantle and the ring, and that you shall live chaste, the two of you?" Bishop Repingdon asked.

"Yes, my lord," John answered meekly. "And in token that we both vow to live chaste, I here offer my hands into yours."

With that, John placed his hands joined in prayer between the bishop's hands. After the bishop spoke a few ancient, sacred words, the carnal marriage of Margery and John Kempe died, reborn anew in celibacy before God. The white clothes, however, were another matter. "Come to dinner a few days hence, and we'll talk then," the bishop said.

On that day, the Kempes sat down in the bishop's dining room with his clerics, who cross-examined Margery. As they ate, Margery stuck to her orthodoxy, wholeheartedly accepting church authority.

After Margery and John left for their inn, the clerics debated the matter. Bishop Repingdon then sent a steward to get Margery and John. "Margery, on advice from my council, you have my blessing for your pilgrimage," he said. Margery grinned.

"But you do not have permission to wear white," Bishop Repingdon said with cool equipoise. Margery grimaced.

"Wait until you come back from Jerusalem, when you have proved yourself and are recognized," he added. Good advice, given the times.

But Margery felt the bishop had constructed a ruse. She got another appointment with the bishop a few days later because Jesus instructed her to give him the following speech.

"You care more about what people will think of you than the perfect love of God," Margery chastised him as Bishop Repingdon sat listening. "For Jesus would have let you fulfill my wish, just as God excused the children of Israel when God ordered them to borrow the goods of the people of Egypt," provisional sins to escape the pharaoh. It was curious reasoning, bending the law to accommodate the good. One of the bishop's clerics eavesdropping outside the door turned to another and said, "Margery would fight with a statue if she could."

A memory. A blunt letter filled with dire warnings a younger, piqued Repingdon had rushed off to King Henry IV more than a decade before, demanding the king clean up his royal court before civil order collapsed.

"Law and justice are exiles from the realm: thefts, homicides, adulteries, fornications, oppressions of the poor, quarrels, and disobedience abound," Repingdon scolded the king. "A tyrannical willfulness replaces the law. The Lord God grows angry day by day."

The bishop met again with his men, who advised, "She claims Jesus told her that those who hear her, hear the voice of God. Move Margery along out of your office," and Repingdon did, his face changed into the lineaments of the smooth courtier. He dispatched Margery the same way the Roman Caesar Claudius might have dealt with minor fistfights in the Camulodunum brick factory.

"In my courteous wisdom, because you are not a member of my diocese, I am not authorized to give you what you desire," Bishop Repingdon told Margery. "Perhaps you could ask a higher power, Archbishop Arundel, to grant you license to wear white and to wear the ring?"

But again she surprised his men by rebuking the bishop, "Sir, I will go to my Lord of Canterbury very willingly, because of other reasons and other matters which I have to confide to his reverence. As for this present reason, I shall not go for that, for God does not wish me to ask the archbishop about it."

Amused, still unoffended, the bishop sent Margery on her way with twenty-six shillings and eight pence, perhaps hoping she would spend the money on a proper pilgrim's outfit. "You should write a book, Margery," he advised, as she stalked away.

CHAPTER SIXTEEN

Arundel, then Julian

The Kempes headed straight to London to see Archbishop Arundel, a round trip of about 175 miles. It was September 1413, and a hot summer had not yet let go of the land. London steamed in a rich, pungent stew of fish, meat, vegetables, flowers, and offal.

At the gates of London, they stopped and got advice from a local yeoman about how best to travel through the city's crowded, labyrinthine streets of poverty and violence, teeming with merchants, fortune seekers, shoppers, and thieves. The Kempes led their ponies past soaring churches, magnificent estates, past public houses. London was home to the sacred and profane, city of royalty, holiness, secrets, and stinks.

The sun was nearing its peak in the sky as the Kempes approached a tavern that was highly recommended, one of 350 in London. Inside, the religious sat elbow to elbow with the ragged swindlers, bankers in ponderous velvet, and rowdy slatterns in lurid satin, some drinking ale caudled with egg yolks, others honey-based drinks, mead or metheglin flavored with herbs. Across the tavern men and women sat licking their fingers from muttonchops or chicken pies, some of the same fingers that in a flash could pickpocket the Kempes.

Margery and John finished eating and walked outside. They continued past the whitewashed arches of London Bridge, as civilians, horses, and wagons jammed the streets. They marveled at the intimidating Tower of London, home to enemies of the throne. They wondered about the builders of the grand St. Paul's Cathedral.

As a mid-afternoon summer sun brightened the rooftops, the Kempes finally arrived in Lambeth Palace's bustling courtyard, filled with knights, grooms, servants, squires, clerics, merchants, and commoners on business with the church. All were rushing to and fro, elbowing each other to get ahead.

Impatient people cut each other in the line, triggering curses, as guards shoved them back. "God be damned of you. I can stand where I want," a man swore.

"By Christ's passion you'll stay on that line where I told you," the guard growled as he pushed the man back. But swearing and taking the Lord's name in vain drew Margery's rage out of her like a wildfire.

With the ramifying power of maternal authority, she chastised the crowd, "Stop swearing. Your cursing injures Jesus himself and you place your immortal souls in peril of damnation."

The crowd was momentarily struck silent, some red-faced. "Who is this woman pretending to be a Lollard preacher, against the law," the guard muttered back.

With lightning rapidity, Margery was branded a heretic by the crowd. Incoherent, blasphemous curses spilled out of their mouths like wheat careening off a runaway wagon. "I wish you were in Smithfield, and I would bring a bundle of sticks to burn you with. It is a pity that you are alive," a woman in a fur cloak said.

But Margery stood stoic, chin out toward the crowd, making them purple with rage.

Finally, a fat esquire wearing a short embroidered gown with sleeves cut long and wide wearily announced, "The wife and husband Kempe." He had watched the spat from a distance with the disinterested look of a French bulldog viewing a fight between a cat and a terrier.

Margery glided through the mob, John in her wake. Into the garden the couple walked, Margery earnest, eagerly looking at Archbishop Arundel's empty, carved oak chair with a red velvet cushion. The archbishop was just now mentioning to his steward, "I am familiar with Margery. I believe I visited with her father, the mayor of Bishop's Lynn."

"You were there in 1409, your grace," the steward said as he helped the archbishop put on his ecclesiastical robes.

"Yes," Arundel said abruptly. The steward, nervous about his too-intimate detail, distracted him, "Margery is a mother of fourteen, but she wears white like a nun. She claims she talks to Jesus." With that, Archbishop Arundel marched out of the room.

The Kempes bowed deeply as England's most powerful religious leader sat down in his chair, his profile gaunt, aquiline. He blankly looked back, intrigued, giving no unnecessary gesture, no hint of emotion.

"Blessed are you, your grace, I pray you a good many days for your generosity in seeing me," Margery began, as John glanced at her sideways.

"Why are you here?" Archbishop Arundel asked, quinine cool.

"I pray your gracious lordship to grant me authority in choosing a confessor," she started, anxiously clearing her throat.

"And?" he asked, eyebrows raised.

"Your grace, I wish to receive communion every Sunday, if God so wishes," she said meekly, hoping to get a blessing for already receiving the Eucharist regularly.

Tired and ill, with only a few months to live, he summoned his clerks to write up Margery's request in a letter carrying his seal, a letter she needed to travel safely. "At no extra fee, and no tips for you either," the archbishop said to them, irked they had to do this paperwork for free.

Now at ease, finding Arundel benign, Margery found the nerve to sally forth. "But your grace, do you find fault in my visions and particularly my public crying, which so many people take offense at?" she asked.

"Explain," the archbishop said.

"I have religious visions and cry for Jesus. I have often begged God to moderate my compunction, but my tears come unbidden," she said, words spilling. "Jesus, though, tells me he gives them to me as he wills, not according to my will, and that I must prepare my body to suffer for him, for the greater glory of God."

"Jesus speaks to her?" thought his aide, watching Arundel. Listening to her explanation, Arundel still saw nothing heretical in Margery.

"I find no fault in you, I approve your manner of living, and am right glad our merciful Lord Jesus Christ shows such grace in our days," the archbishop said.

Margery was overjoyed. But then she overstepped, perhaps thinking of the vulgar, fur-clad woman in the hall who had slandered her. Margery drew herself up and told Arundel, "My lord, our Lord of all, almighty God, has not given you your benefice and great worldly wealth in order to maintain those who are traitors to him, and those who slay him every day by the swearing of great oaths. You shall answer for them to God, unless you correct them or else put them out of your service."

Arundel's mind stopped like a tree branch in a wagon wheel. He sat bolt upright, his now unsmiling, scissored profile perched forward atop his bulky cloaks. Arundel was used to having the sleeve of his robes yanked on by the beseeching faithful, but not a presumptuous laywoman attacking him for running a wild, disorderly household. A woman preaching against oaths, talking publicly of the Gospel, criticizing clerics? All hallmarks of Lollardy. His mood hardened.

A flashback. Seven years prior, the Lollard knights had deliberately turned their backs on Arundel parading by with his clerics holding the Eucharist aloft, and instead continued chatting. Seething, a younger Arundel chastised King Henry IV, "Henry, there is abomination in your court I think no one has ever seen among Christians. Your rule will not last if your disgraceful knights continue to undermine the Blessed Sacrament."

Agonizing moments ticked by. But after a time Arundel calmed down and replied, "I agree." Information about misdoings in his backyard was always good to have. Surprised by his equanimity, their ensuing conversation struck concordant notes.

As they talked, Margery increasingly endeared herself to Arundel. She was a student of an author Arundel was fond of, the Carthusian Nicholas Love, whose translation of *The Mirror of the Blessed Life of Jesus Christ* had an anti-Lollard appendix on the Blessed Sacrament that Arundel had authorized for use in the church's campaign against heretics.

As guards redirected those on line to other officials, Margery and Arundel talked for hours about religious works, amid the breezes of a clement south wind until stars glowed in the night sky.

But even Archbishop Arundel's support wasn't enough. The potential for a ferocious backlash against a married woman in white traveling alone was that serious. So Margery decided to visit England's most famous mystic and one if its greatest theologians, who revolutionized Christianity with profound new insights about sin, heaven, and hell that she said came from Jesus himself. Margery visited Julian of Norwich.

Julian was an anchorite connected to the church in Norwich. She counseled people through her window with such humble compassion, grace, and raw purity that Christians from all over England and Europe came in droves to her cell. As a young girl, Julian had witnessed unspeakable suffering as the Black Death turned England into a graveyard. Later, spiritual doubts afflicted Julian in her twenties.

A severe illness put Julian on the brink of death in 1373, the same year Margery was born. Wracked with pain, her body covered in sweat, Julian laid in bed dying for eight days. Nursemaids raced to and fro, changing her wet bed linens, putting cold compresses on her forehead.

But during the final two days of her illness, Julian laid in bed meekly listening as Jesus gave her complex visitations, or showings, rich with profound meaning, messages she was still trying to discern before she died in 1416. In and around 1393, the same year Margery almost died in childbirth, Julian's visions were written down in what is thought to be one of the greatest works of Christian mysticism, *The Sixteen Revelations of Divine Love.*

In the smothering darkness, Julian hung out a lantern fired by the optimistic theology of the God of Love. She spoke of a God whose will shall be worked throughout creation, that the madness of earth is not the end of the story, a message characteristically English in its spirituality and common sense. Suffering was not God's vengeful wrath on mankind. Instead, God is simply about mercy, love, and compassion, a truth arrived at through, surprisingly, sin. Anger exists only in humans struck through with blindness. Know the limits of human understanding which cannot grasp the ultimate reality, and trust, as Julian said Christ had told her, that "all shall be well, and all shall be well, and all manner of things shall be well."

By the time Margery visited Julian, the mystic was approaching seventy and slowly becoming untethered from earth. Margery knocked on Julian's door. Fasting had hollowed out her cheeks, and her nerves had plowed furrows in her forehead.

Julian slid open her window in her door and waited. She had seen women like this before, talkative, anxious, a woman searching for Jesus out in the world while Julian was searching inward. Margery then poured out her soul, her past sins, her grief over them. "My visions, are they divinely inspired or not? Is there any deceit in them?" she asked.

Julian answered simply, "The Holy Ghost never urges a thing against charity, and if he did, he would be contrary to his own self, for he is all charity." The mystic added, "He that is forever doubting is like the wave of the sea which is moved and borne about with the wind, and that man is not likely to receive the gifts of God."

Margery asked, "But what about my crying over Christ's death?"

Julian advised, "When God visits a creature with tears of contrition, devotion, or compassion, he may and ought to believe that the Holy Ghost is in his soul," adding, "no evil spirit may give these tokens. The devil has no power in a man's soul."

Still Margery was worried about the gossips, "What about unbelievers who doubt my piety, saying I am a false hypocrite?"

Julian replied, "Do not fear the talk of the world, for the more contempt, shame and reproof that you have in this world, the more is your merit in the sight of God. Patience is necessary for you, for in that shall you keep your soul."

Margery spent a number of days getting comfort from Julian, and would later say, "Every good thought is a speech of God."

CHAPTER SEVENTEEN

Pilgrimage

*A*utumn came, it was time for Margery to go on pilgrimage to the Holy Land, her dream realized.

Fr. Spryngolde, Margery's confessor, took to the pulpit one Sunday at her request and asked the congregation whether the Kempes owed anyone any money so they could be repaid before she left. Just as Jesus ordered, Margery needed to be in charity with everyone to avoid lengthening time in purgatory in case she died along the way.

Later, Fr. Spryngolde took her aside, intending to give Margery comfort but instead mystifying her, "I had a vision that you would suffer along the way, that your fellow pilgrims and your handmaid will abandon you, but rescue will come in the form of a broken-backed man who will lead you to safety."

At home, Margery bustled about the house, as John and the children stood by wondering, anxious. She would be gone for nearly two years. John had resigned himself to the pilgrimage. Their friends would help him take care of the children, who somehow managed to take care of each other.

Guidebooks at the time were full of advice on what to buy. That included a featherbed, two little traveling pillows, two pairs of sheets, and a quilt. Linen undergarments were good to keep cool, and a roomy, cozy top cloak was needed out on the ocean at night.

They advised to pack a knife, spoon, bowl, candles, comb, leather flask, and a St. Christopher's medal. Digestifs and ginger syrup were recommended because the cold north of England had bred a people not used to the mercurial, Mediterranean trade winds that delivered all sorts of bacteria. Food at sea was notoriously starchy and constipating, so laxatives such as figs and cloves should be packed. All could be carried in a bucket, which was handy because the pail could be used both for food storage and for bouts of seasickness.

Most important, the guidebooks admonished to keep everyone as a friend at sea, to not be immoderate or untactful, the wisdom of small favors. Thieves targeted pilgrims hiding in hedgerows or forests, as did shipmates or even fellow pilgrims.

Margery shopped in town. She got a bucket to store her haul of cheese, biscuits, boiled eggs, dried fruit, fish and meat, and wine, less prone to spoiling than water.

"Margery," John said as he touched her shoulder while she was bent over packing her bags. She looked up, and they hugged each other tightly, as their toddlers climbed up their knees.

A day later, a wagon pulled up in front to take Margery and her maid on the first step of their journey. She kissed her husband and children, walked out of the house, stepped up onto the wagon, and turned around waving good-bye, as John stood in the doorway holding their children on either side.

After they made an offering at the Cathedral of the Holy Trinity in Norwich for protection, Margery and her maid headed to Yarmouth, made another offering to an image of the Blessed Mother, and then went to meet the captain of their ship, now busy mapping out the journey.

First a grueling voyage over the choppy, grey North Sea to Zierikzee in the Netherlands. A town friendly to Bishop's Lynn, it imported Lynn's wool and exported herring and other goods into England via

Lynn. From Zierikzee, the pilgrims would head south to Constance, a sparkling city at the western end of Lake Constance on the border of Germany and Switzerland, where church leaders were just now gathering to stop the papal schism. They would then continue past Constance overland to Bologna and Venice, and grab a ship in Venice to sail to the Holy Land. The trip from Bishop's Lynn to Venice would take about a month and a half.

The captain on the dock looked up, a good-natured smile creasing his weathered cheeks as Margery and her maid walked toward him. He wrote down their information on the ship's manifest pressed against his knee-length, brown wool gown.

Margery glanced behind him at his twin-masted boat rocking in the swells off the dock. The hulk was up to date, a hundred feet long, with a large square sail hung from a yardarm on the main mast, bonnet sails at bottom to increase the power of the larger sail. The captain's quarters were in the back at the stern, a hammock slung between wood-paneled walls, a lamp nearby.

Other pilgrims, all from Bishop's Lynn or Norfolk, walked up. "Very good men," Margery thought. Initially, that is. One would oversee the common purse, another the daily meals, two a day. Still another would track the route overland to get to Venice.

But the captain was key. He must be strong and keep strict order on the ship; even minor distractions could quickly snuff out their lives at sea. Margery had also brought along a secret terror she dared not share with anyone: a profound fear of drowning, no tombstone to visit, no flowers or love notes to leave, just eternal, icy darkness.

Margery decided she would help the captain keep order. But as she went back to get her things on the dock, a ferocious brawl broke out. His crew of newly hired shipmates tried to clamor aboard after demanding too high wages. The captain grabbed one by the collar so hard he nearly strangled him with it. "By God's holy teeth, you shall not get on my boat, you calf pizzle, unless you agree to this wage," he said.

A deckhand muttered back, "By Satan's hairy arse, we shall."

Another yelped, "If you don't pay us, we will curse your fat-bellied tosspot for a drunkard that you are, right to hell."

But eradicating cursing was her charism, and nothing would stop her from that even if God dropped a hook from heaven to reel her in. "Enough," Margery yelled, stopping them cold. "Cease your swearing. You are in great disfavor with God." The deckhands and the pilgrims stood up, startled a woman was yelling at a crowd of men.

Meanwhile, Guy had just arrived on the dock with Ruth. He was going alone on this pilgrimage. Guy had daydreamed for months about this trip, as he was leaving behind his scold of a wife. He was the sole focus of her daily hectoring because they didn't have children, and Guy didn't want anything spoiling it.

Gilbert then showed up on the dock. He was going on pilgrimage to escape his creditors, believing he could avoid paying the bills for his tannery for months on end. A furious cobbler in town demanded, "You have owed me money since last June. When will you pay me back?"

"How about Noctober?" Gilbert chortled, and ran away. The situation was made worse when Gilbert was practicing with his bow and arrow, shooting at rats in the town dump, and accidentally shot the cobbler in the leg as he walked by on the street beyond.

Meanwhile, Margery was still holding forth, her maid standing by, listening, "All of you who journey with me must attend to the Good Word every day and behave at the highest level of Christian perfection in everything you do, all with good manners."

Guy said to Gilbert as they loaded their things on to the boat, "I'm so thrilled to have a woman on board preaching while we're vomiting miles out at sea. Words escape me."

To Guy and Gilbert, travel was all about irresponsibility and letting go, their only redeeming quality a holy curiosity. Now, unexpectedly, Margery was about to ruin it for them, turning their fun into feelings of moral shabbiness. It would be as if they were stuck with their in-laws in a closet for months on end.

Fr. Donald suddenly showed up on the dock and announced he was joining their pilgrim party. Fr. Spryngolde had asked him to stand in as Margery's confessor. He would be to her soul like "a smith with a file makes the iron bright and clear." Margery gave him a wary look. She still trusted Fr. Donald, believing he would support her. Even though behind her back Fr. Donald hotly contested her intimate, familiar relations with Jesus coming so soon after her quick conversion from her sinful past.

The pilgrims lugged on board cages of live chickens to lay eggs, wooden crates of crabs and oysters, casks of wine and ale, barrels of salted fish, dried fruit, bread, and cheese. Guy felt for his bag of almonds he would later mash into milk for the journey, then joined the others as they climbed down the rope ladder to the bottom of the bucket, to the cramped hold below deck.

Unmellowed pine resin comforted them at first. But then a gust of hot air hit them full in the face. After racing to find their berths, they settled in and tried to get comfortable, looking around. No portholes here, the hold was airtight, lest the ship's hull was breached and they were all spilt out of a seam into the ocean. The only light and air came to them from up above or through the hatchways. The lavatory was either a pail in the back behind a door, near the animal pens, or it was a long bench behind doors that hung out over the water on either side of the rudder.

In the close quarters, Margery prayed, "Lord, drive away my enemies and preserve my chastity." She was bound to Christ now. Anything less would be a direct offense against her heavenly spouse.

As the boat rocked against the walls of the dock, the captain took the helm and barked commands. The deck hands untied the mooring rope and pulled the lines in, as others raced to hike up the main sail. Workers just up ahead on the dock lifted the chain across the entrance of the port.

The bladder of the ship's sail ballooned forward. The creaking wood groaned as the prow rose up over the mount of the open sea and then fell into a watery trough, a wave breaking over the figurehead of the mermaid's head. As the boat righted itself, the canvas of the sail sounded a crack as herring gulls, piping plovers, and sea gulls hurriedly crowded overhead to accompany the boat out of the port, the sun full blast in the captain's face as he searched for the sea roads up ahead.

On deck, Margery would constantly search for the telltale spoke of lightning and black storms charring the horizon, listening for detonating thunder. Pilgrims often found Margery on her knees at her berth, praying to Jesus or St. Erasmus, protector of ships in storms.

Despite petty quarrels, the pilgrims were quiet for the first leg of the voyage, playing games or music, dangling their arms over the railing as the water rushed by, their faces up to the sun.

A few weeks in, Guy and Margery sat up in the dead of night and looked at each other from across the way, awakened by shouts from up above in the deep darkness. Something was terribly wrong.

Then a sickening plunge of the boat, and the two looked at each other in sheer terror. The boat had entered mountainous seas made huge by a hurricane west wind, and had just taken a gut-clenching, twenty-foot dive down the sheer face of a wave. The strakes of the hulk, overlapping planks of caulked wood, were working hard to stay together, evincing a hideous, piercing noise as the timbers scraped against each other. The ship was about to wrench itself apart at sea.

Margery looked into Guy's eyes and immediately understood. They were about to become just another long forgotten story in Bishop's Lynn, a sorry, self-satisfied tale told of silly pilgrims drowned at sea. "Lash yourselves to the timbers," Guy shouted at the pilgrims now awakening, as he battened down a sleeping Gilbert with ropes, helping Margery, too.

Terrified, they sat white-knuckled holding on to the pillars and stared up at the ceiling, trying to discern the shouts ripped out to sea by the howling wind.

Hours passed as the captain and his crew fought the storm. It was only at dawn that it blew away, the waters calm again. Finally, the captain laid down his exhausted head, uneasy in his hammock, and slept for most of the morning. Margery and the pilgrims walked about on the deck in dazed silence, for the first time understanding how dangerous this trip really was.

Later that evening, as twilight passed into night and the pilgrims went to bed, Margery secretly climbed to the upper deck, using each rung as a rosary bead in gratitude for the captain and the crew. She then stowed herself in a corner, getting great comfort silently watching the captain as he gave hushed, murmured orders, his silhouette edged by starlight as he safely guided their ship across acres of watery, moonlit ocean.

• • •

Battling Pilgrims

A grey morning a few days later, the ship finally landed in the port town of Zierikzee, the jostling awakening the pilgrims below. They lugged their things to the deck above, thanked the captain and crew, and then met on the dock to hash out the next leg of their journey, which would take them through Cologne, Mainz, Strasbourg, and Basel.

The plan was to find a river heading south and follow it mostly on foot. They would walk along beside rivers like the Rhine, or through muddy, slippery creek beds, searching for the deep tracks of hidden roads previous wayfarers had laid down, often blocked by downed trees. They would travel fifteen miles a day, the average rate to travel.

While in Zierikzee, Margery went to the church of St. Lieven, a splendid cathedral with forty-nine altars. Margery received the Eucharist there with tremendous sobbing, to the point of perspiring through her white mantle. She was crying for her own sins and the rest of the pilgrims as well.

Back at the local inn, the others scowled at her in silence. Guy muttered, "The Londinium aqueduct authority could have used her waterworks."

"All about the love and goodness of our Lord, yes, fine," said Gilbert. "But even at the table, or even when we are trying to sleep?"

"You all ought to be mindful that you are supposed to behave as good men," Margery said to their backs, not hearing their answers as they headed to their rooms.

Through the icy mud of the eastern front they continued toward Constance, under the broadening blue sky of the northern hemisphere, meeting along the way other pilgrim parties with horses dragging wagons covered in painted canvases, which carried either their things or women pilgrims. All the while talking, fighting, carrying on, declaiming, harassing, being kind, then starting in all over again. About ten miles outside Constance, things blew up.

All this time, the pilgrims had kept Margery in the back of the group, even though she had repeatedly broken through to lecture about the Gospels. One morning, the pilgrims held an impromptu meeting over breakfast at the inn about Margery.

"Another bout of excessive crying yesterday. And lecturing," said Guy, as Margery knelt upstairs in her room, praying.

"Oh hush now, she'll be quiet if you ask her," said another pilgrim, James, inclined to defend Margery out of kindness.

Fr. Donald stared them into silence. Then he spoke, the light on the Damascus Road, "She is the woman riding on the red beast in the Apocalypse who will open the seals for all of our damnation if we don't stop her."

The pilgrims looked back puzzled. But James understood where he was headed: banishment.

"If I agreed with you, Father, then we'd both be wrong," James said, as Fr. Donald stared back, stumped. He was about to blast him when Guy interrupted.

"Steadfastness under persecution, Father, isn't that our way to perfection?" Guy mocked.

But Fr. Donald was just getting started. He slicked back his mink-smooth tonsure, pleased with his pleasant, brilliant nature. Fr. Donald had told his bishop at home, who rolled his eyes, "I desire only the wisdom of a silent pilgrim's road."

"Margery has not eaten meat for four years, defying my orders," Fr. Donald said. "Even the mystic Richard Rolle said excessive fasting is as sinful as gluttony. It makes one heretically dualist, that food is evil."

James interjected, "Rolle was a lunatic, running off into the woods in his sister's nightgown, cutting the sleeves off."

But Fr. Donald berated him, "He was making a rochet, you idiot, the surplice of a priest."

Then Guy said, "Yes, that's it, you can beat yourself with holly brambles and wear hedgehog fur, but if you try to achieve grace through only your will, you increase only in vainglory."

Fr. Donald nodded, "Ascetism is her vainglory. Margery cannot become sacred through her own self, but only through the grace of God."

Guy agreed, "Then at minimum she must eat meat and drink again, if she won't be abstemious in her lecturing and sobbing."

Later, at lunch at the main dining table in the inn, Fr. Donald scolded Margery as she lectured from *Pilgrim's Progress*, "I order you to eat meat and drink wine and ale again, and to shut up," as he clapped his hands over his ears.

But then Fr. Donald remembered himself. He spoke softly, his eyes falsely round, "Please, dear Margery, join us at table."

But Margery shook her head no, "The love and goodness of our Lord is great." Fr. Donald may as well have been shouting into a snowdrift.

"Margery, please remember, you are not in England anymore," James whispered to her.

She ignored him and said, "You are all displeased because I weep so much and speak always of the love and goodness of our

Lord, at the table and in other places."

Guy interrupted her, "We will not suffer you as your husband did when you were at home in England."

But Margery rebuked him, "Our Lord, Almighty God, is as great a Lord here as in England, and I have as great cause to love him here as there."

Gilbert snapped, "No wonder your husband didn't come with you."

Margery quietly answered, "I only greatly desire your love, if I might have it by God's pleasure. You cause me much shame and hurt."

Gilbert interrupted, "You make all of us unhappy. You are ruining this pilgrimage for us all."

As Margery got up and left the table, Guy yelled at her back, "I pray God that the devil's wrath may overtake you soon and quickly." Margery stayed separate from them for the rest of the day.

There were more troubling things worrying the pilgrims. They had heard rumors of the Pope's public condemnation of Wyclif and the Bohemian heretic he inspired, Jan Hus, and increasingly feared that Margery's extravagant, public displays would put them in danger, that Constance city officials might mistakenly think they were a renegade band of heretics escaping from England.

The pilgrims made a decision at the breakfast table the next morning. "Depart, go your own way," they told Margery in her room at the inn. She was stunned, then quietly began to cry.

The group found separate lodgings in another town just a day's journey from Constance, and off to bed they went, Guy muttering into his pillow, "To be made mindful that we are sinners every second is an unbearable penance."

The next morning, James took Margery aside and advised, "With all humility ask our fellowship if you might still travel in our company."

So she did, her head bowed to the ground. The pilgrims shuffled their feet and looked down, too. The group felt ashamed at how they had mistreated Margery. "Would we be good Christians if we threw her out in the middle of strangers?" asked Guy at supper.

"Maybe Margery is a penance for our sins," Gilbert said.

Later they met with her. "At dinnertime, you will sit at the end of the table, beneath all the others, and stay silent," ordered Guy. "And only in Constance. After that, you are on your own."

One morning soon after, the pilgrims sat at breakfast hung over, their heads throbbing like a blacksmith's anvil. Margery was still turning everything into a lecture. When she started to talk to another pilgrim about the Gospel according to Luke, Guy hit his limit. As she walked by, Guy seized her, and as Gilbert held her arms, he cut her white gown with a table knife so short that it fell just below the knee. The two then put a canvas sackcloth over Margery's head and yanked it down around her waist, like an apron, as she started to cry.

"You are a business woman, a brewer, and a miller, remember?" Guy said to Margery's face now tensed red from tears. "This apron will show the world what you truly are and not the holier than thou saint in waiting you pretend to be."

Margery's chest heaved. "I don't want to wear this," she said, her voice dry, letting out a tiny cough. But they were in an unforgiving mood.

"We'll let the apron be white, to show your purity," Guy said.

Resigned, Margery kept silent, sitting in her new place at the end of the dinner table, wearing her new costume. A nervous, awkward calm settled on the pilgrims that night as they ate a dinner of mortrews, chicken and pork with breadcrumbs, powder forte, sugar, saffron, and salt.

Then the pilgrims' malice backfired on them. When they heard of the bullying and saw her new costume, local townspeople and owners of the lodgings they arrived at felt sorry for her. They invited Margery to their tables, only angering the pilgrims more. "You will be attacked yourselves if you don't stop attacking her," they warned Guy and Gilbert, but the two ignored them.

The next day, after a breakfast of hard cheese, eggs, and tough bread, they gathered their things and started walking. In the afternoon, Constance gleamed in the distance. The travelers heaved a sigh of relief as they gazed upon this glittering town perched on an isthmus jutting into a lake rippling with sunlight, graceful church spires piercing the sky.

Margery thought it was the most wonderful place she had ever seen. Guy thought, "This is the perfect place to leave her behind." Unbeknownst to the pilgrims, it was also a city where right now, intrigue lurked in every corner.

CHAPTER NINETEEN

Abandoned

Around the time Margery's pilgrim party arrived in Constance, Archbishop Arundel lay dying. But the council was still choosing a pope and pursuing heretics, even those dead for decades. A year later it would decree Wyclif a heretic, ordering his body exhumed and burnt, his ashes cast into the River Swift in England. It also condemned to death the heretics Jan Hus of Bohemia and Jerome of Prague.

After a few days in Constance, Margery became worried because she needed to make a confession. She found an English friar, the pope's legate in the city, and sat down with him, meek as any housewife who had just endured a season's worth of shocking insults. Seeing she was devout, the friar vowed his support.

Afterward, the pilgrims invited the legate to dinner. "Perhaps you could look into this troublesome matter?" Fr. Donald asked delicately, referring to Margery, as the legate gave him a thin smile.

At the table, Margery's fellow pilgrims relaxed and started to speak freely. "Pilgrimages are dangerous enough even without this constant public weeping," Guy confided to the legate off to the side, pretending he knew they were both sophisticated world travelers. Listening quietly, the friar finally stood up.

"No, sirs, I will not make her eat meat while she can abstain and be the better disposed to love our Lord," he said. "Whichever of you all who made a vow to walk to Rome barefoot, I would not dispense him of his vow whilst he might fulfill it." As for Margery's crying, he added, "It is not in my power to restrain it, for it is the gift of the Holy Ghost."

The legate thought for another minute, then gave a compromise freighted with a severe warning, "As for her talking, I will ask her to stop until she comes somewhere that people will hear her more gladly than you do."

At first dumbstruck, the pilgrims grew incensed. "Then you be in charge of her. We want nothing more to do with her," said Guy. "Even her maid wants to stay with us," glaring Margery's maid into submission.

Gilbert said, "Here, here is all of her money in the treasury: twenty pounds."

So Margery was abandoned. She counted the money and saw the group had wrongfully kept an extra sixteen pounds of her funds. But she couldn't do anything about it because they already had left.

Margery went to pray in a local church for help and protection. She got up and stepped out of the dark gloom of the church, temporarily blinded by sunlight. Across the way stood an old man with a white beard. He stepped forward. "My name is William Weaver. I am a guide for hire. I see your fellow Englishmen have rejected you," he said.

"Where are you from?" Margery, delighted, asked.

"Devonshire. I am ready to assist you for a daily wage," he said. They struck a deal. Now Margery wanted vindication.

Knocking on Guy's door at the inn, Margery announced, triumphant, to the gathering within, "I have made other arrangements. God is with me, and I shall not fail. However, you might fail, because God in his infinite mercy showed me in a vision that it would be so." The message was clear. They were in mortal danger.

"Yes, and that old man will put up quite a fight against the thieves and rapists along the way," Gilbert joked to Guy, who chuckled.

Worse, neither Margery nor William Weaver spoke a lick of any foreign tongue, including Italian. As they left town, soon William began to complain about his various aches and pains due to his age. "I am afraid you shall be taken from me, and I shall be beaten because of you and my coat will be stolen," he said.

"William, don't be afraid, God will look after us very well," Margery said, still deeply anxious.

The two headed south on a track that would take them past the lowest part of the Swiss Alps toward Venice, following a path spotted with deep moss that led through woods dating back centuries, a roof of giant ferns and evergreen trees overhead. They walked for weeks, circumventing craggy, forested hills even rabbits couldn't pass through.

On many mornings, her face held high in the driving rain, Margery looked up to the sky, thought of the woman accused of adultery in the Gospels, and prayed to God to protect her and her chastity. At night they would stop and take shelter in any abandoned barn or cave they could find. Somehow, William could light a gorging fire anywhere with flinty rocks. One night, they threw a log on the fire outside an abandoned hut they had found, and Margery blew on the coals, the wilderness and its mystery surrounding them, as they fell asleep.

The next day at noon, the two approached a rising hilltop and looked down into a valley of ice-bound forests, then up into the sky and fell silent. Through looming mountain paths they crept for hours as the afternoon sun started to wane, the wind picking up. Margery and William only had so much daylight time to travel, since night dropped quickly in this part of the world. Other pilgrim travelers had already warned them that if they wandered around in the dark, they might step out into thin air and plunge head over heels to their deaths.

Soon tidal waves of shattering cold blasted through their lungs as Margery and William grabbed at rock walls on the sides of them to get by, stopping for shelter in the cleft of huge evergreen trees blown open by storms from long ago. After a bit, William grabbed her shoulder and pointed ahead.

The valley had opened into a cozy basin ringed by gorgeous, white-capped mountains, lit with a majestic orange glow. The world felt wide. The sky was hitting new heights. "Just the sight of this could make anyone feel giant, Promethean," William said, as Margery looked in wonderment at him.

After a while, William said, "Winter is a season of feeling alive, and yet nature literally lies down. But soon, spring will lower itself from the perfect into our cold, dark world and renew us again, just as Jesus did."

Later, they found a cave to sleep in and reverently looked up into the amphitheater of the Milky Way towering above them, a whirl-wind of constellations and meteor showers. In the stormy magnetic flux, comets were being reshaped into moons and jumbo planets that Nicholas, the astronomer back home in Bishop's Lynn, peered up at, too, divining their Euclidean aspects in the night sky, fear and faith in the dark between. Comforted, Margery and William made camp for the night and soon fell asleep.

When day broke over the mountains, they sat up, their limbs stiff, the hard, cold ground feeling like a brass bed. After they finished eating, they bundled their things together and started walking again, past rushing mountain streams, past rocks of quartz and feldspar, skylarks hovering.

Later, the two joined a party of pilgrims loaded into a wagon pulled by a couple of gigantic horses. Finally they were making rapid time. They crossed into Italy, a country that didn't really seem like a country, but a fractious, teeming peninsula pushed and pulled on all sides by infighting and five oceans and seas.

They stayed a week in Bologna, the main city of trade between the north and Venice. Margery was so entertaining at the inns in town that Swiss and Italian women let her sleep in their beds so they could carry on their conversations.

One morning a few days later, Margery turned around at the breakfast table and saw off in the distance what looked like a weary band of travelers wearing familiar clothes.

CHAPTER TWENTY

Unexpected Reunion

Her former group of pilgrims had arrived, and they were dumb-struck that Margery had beaten them with just an old man as her guide.

"Maybe God really is protecting her, and will protect us, too, if we take her back in," Gilbert said to Guy, both ambivalent as they sat in the public house.

"Or maybe Elijah scooped her up in his winged chariot, and they flew here," Guy said, thoroughly aggravated and now more so with Gilbert.

Thinking Guy was playing with him, Gilbert said, "Or maybe she rode in on Sir Gawain's Gringolet. I feel poetic."

As Guy was about to smack him, James interrupted, "Mouse brains, God is protecting her. How can Margery be evil when she always observes her prayers and confession?"

Guy bit back, "I will not countenance traveling with a woman who acts like she carries the Holy of Holies in her womb." But behind his back, Gilbert cajoled Margery's maid into inviting her back in, hoping God could include them in Margery's wingspan of protection. As William went his own way, she agreed, but on one condition set by the leader of the pilgrims.

"You will not talk of the Gospel where we are, but you will sit still and make merry, like us, at all meals," Guy ordered her.

Margery glumly gave in, but then perked up with a caveat, "I will make merry, but not from vanity of mind, abhorrent to me, but from a cheerful conscience that will buoy my spirits and yours."

Guy grimaced. "Freedom of conscience is still free will to find you intolerable," he said to her as they turned in for the night.

The pilgrims were awakened the next morning by the dogs guarding their packhorses barking at unseen thieves in the woods nearby. "Feed and water them," Guy ordered Gilbert and James. They rubbed down the horses they had picked up along the way and led them out onto the melting surface of a nearby pond to break up the thick ice to drink, a cold spring in the air. The pilgrims then trimmed their luggage to their packsaddles and wagons, and started out again.

Finally, after two months, they made it to Venice, where they would stay more than three months. It was May 1414. The pilgrims' feud was nothing compared to the blood vendettas between Italy's city-states. The people of Italy were the most quarrelsome of Europe and yet the most artistic. The countryside was dotted with gorgeous buildings filled with sublime oil paintings, ancient statues, and frescoes depicting famous battles.

Arriving by boat, Margery and the pilgrims looked around, astounded. The city was like nothing they had ever seen. London at that time had at most thirty thousand to forty thousand citizens. But Venice had double that number, cheek to jowl on a string of islands.

Margery fought to contain herself and to not alienate her reacquainted friends, because she wanted nothing to get in the way of seeing the sights. Venice was second to Rome for its extraordinary cathedrals. It, too, was a tourist attraction due to its numerous relics housed in stunning reliquaries studded with priceless gems.

It boasted the holiest relic in the city, a piece of the True Cross, surrounded by oil paintings by artists such as Bellini. Other churches touted a piece of the sponge used to wipe Christ's face on the cross, the knife used by Jesus to slice bread at the Last Supper, the basin Jesus had used to turn water into wine, and St. Mary Magdalene's breastbone, tooth, and comb.

Other churches displayed the body of Mark the Evangelist, (though his head somehow stayed behind in Alexandria, Egypt), the head of the apostle James the Lesser, and the thumb of the Roman emperor Constantine who had legalized the new religion that worshiped the Man of Men. St. Mark's Cathedral was where pilgrims could also see the silver sheath holding the arm bone of St. George.

Venice opened its arms to pilgrims. The city had cornered the lucrative market on tours to the Holy Land. Margery and the pilgrims approached a tour guide on duty in the Piazza San Marco. He knew English and told them where to convert currency and find good inns. As the pilgrims got their things off the boat, Gilbert said, "For the love of Mother Mary, I can't find my pillow." Margery reprimanded him, "Do not blaspheme."

Rolling his eyes, Gilbert looked to Guy, who was commandeering things while sitting on a rickety wooden stool. Here was the sanctimonious Christian lecturing again. Their time in Venice would be ruined if Margery was not reined in.

"By Christ's blood, woman, it is an established law of nature to hate those who chastise and oppress," Guy said.

"It is God's law that we should not curse," Margery fired back.

"Margery, do you know why Lucifer fell," Guy said, standing up in bardic style, an ironic smile curling his lips as he grabbed a big metal hook and stuck it under the rope binding of their luggage.

"Don't say the devil's name. You'll rot out our food and sour the milk," warned Gilbert.

Margery set her mouth thinly to one side, one hand on her hip jutting forward, as she pushed back up her white gable hood falling over her left eye, waiting to be teased.

"Lucifer didn't fall without reason," Guy said. "He literally fell because he wanted peace and quiet, which none of the angels understood."

Gilbert roared with laughter, "Aha, Margery, you are leading us to hell. You make us want to be alone."

Guy ignored him and continued, "Lucifer didn't lead astray the other fallen angels. It was they who followed him. They were mesmerized by the fact that he wanted to be left alone. And that's the true story behind Lucifer's fall from heaven."

But James stopped them, "Your story proves you are an idiot, Guy, and so is Satan. It still shows the true, hateful reason why Satan fell, because he was motivated by his own angry selfishness."

As Guy stepped toward him, James stood up bolder, "Do you really think that, by condemning others, you can wipe out awareness of your own sins? Do you really think that you can force everyone to adapt to your appetites just like the Pharisees believed? Your true nature is betrayed by that planet sticking out over your belt. Get thee behind me, fat one."

Guy lunged at James, who easily darted away. Meanwhile, Margery had already left them behind, heading to the Benedictine convent of San Zaccaria, which was filled with relics, even the whole body of the father of John the Baptist, St. Zacharias.

The other pilgrims split up. Some went to the local souvenir shops, which had a roaring trade in relics. Others went to the section of town where merchants sold all sorts of precious jewels: emerald, amethyst, topaz, sardonyx, and jacinth. Guy picked up a sapphire to let it catch the light.

Farmers came rowing in with butter, cheese, fruit, vegetables, wine, and chickens. The only sources of fresh water were the cisterns on the rooftops or barges on the river Brenta that collected the rain. Although Venetians were considered the most sophisticated in all of Italy, they stunk.

"Do you notice that the people smell like low tide?" Fr. Donald asked an English friar.

"There isn't enough fresh water, so they always smell of perfume and the ocean," the friar replied, as Fr. Donald held a pomander to his nose.

After a while, Margery couldn't keep silent any longer, not in a city with so many churches. At supper a few days later, she again quoted a text from the Bible.

Guy smashed his fork on the table. "You have broken your vow to not teach the Gospel," he fumed.

But Margery drew herself up and said just as loudly, "I can no longer keep this agreement with you, for I must speak of my Lord Jesus Christ, though all this world had forbidden me."

Guy ordered, "You are no longer welcome here. Leave at once." Margery was thrown out again. She ate alone in her room at the hostel for the next few weeks, until it was time to leave.

. . .

The Holy Land

*I*t was now time for the group to move on from Venice. The pilgrims hired a sea captain registered with the city who would then take them first to Jaffa, the port of the Holy Land. Copies of contracts were given to Venice officials, covering meals, inns, and fees for guides in the Holy Land, which the captain would enforce.

The traveling party hurried about gathering their things, shopping in the piazzas near St. Mark's Cathedral. They met on the docks, excited, faces flushed, and reviewed their lists at the staging post, checking off food and wine.

But Margery suddenly ditched their boat in favor of another, after the Lord warned her it was unsuitable. Taking no chances, they switched to Margery's galley, paying the first captain in wine to calm him down.

And so they began a leg of the journey so harrowing, it could only be embarked on twice a year, in spring and autumn. They would be stuck on a month-long trip at sea with a woman more than ready with round-the-clock sermons, who had won their every battle to get rid of her.

Margery had selected well. This new captain was a veteran seaman with fiendish, quicksilver judgment who could find open sea lanes anywhere. Though he was a cussing sailor, the captain was trustworthy. The Saracens knew him, and he knew how to handle them.

His large, two-masted ship, a galley, sat swaying in steady pulses to the waves.

Galleys had rowers that could get them out of trouble at sea, sitting in huge, spacious holds below deck. The pilgrims were also heartened to see that the captain had nearly two-dozen archers on board, ready to fight pirates.

On deck, the pilgrims waved good-bye to the townspeople of Venice standing on the dock. With the rowers pulling to the beat of the drum, the galley climbed up the swell of the harbor's threshold and glided down, then set out for open sea, ripping toward Jerusalem, Star of the East.

The captain had his deckhands chalk out spaces in the cabins below for each pilgrim, which became their homes on the boat. The pilgrims settled down in the cabin below the rowing deck. Margery looked around. Again, no portholes through which they could catch a sea breeze. Chickens and other small animals were vomiting and defecating in their pens. "It is smoldering hot and stinking," Margery said.

The captain followed the same Venetian trade routes that had been followed for centuries. First they would hug the coast of Dalmatia, wind around the Peloponnese, then zip past the Greek islands of Crete, Rhodes, and Cyprus. After the bitter, biting cold of the Swiss Alps, the pilgrims welcomed the lukewarm trade winds puffing at them off the Mediterranean coasts, sailing through blue-green seas with jade underbellies.

A few days later, Margery went to get her bed things. All of the travelers were told to roll up their bed sheets and mattresses each morning and hang them by a rope from a nail at the front of their sleeping cabins. But she was upset to find her sheets stolen by Fr. Donald who wanted to use them as a curtain because he didn't want anyone seeing him undress.

A fight broke out. "The sheet is mine," he said, chin up.

Margery said, "I take God as my witness that this is my sheet."

As the pilgrims gathered, Fr. Donald retorted, "Margery lies." He thought to himself as he stalked away, taking refuge in the abstract again, "What is sin out at sea anyway, but a left-handed form of survival."

Beaten back, Margery laid down only with her cloak to cover her. The next morning, even though she was the victim, Margery could see she had few defenders at the breakfast table. Trying to change the mood against her, she ventured, "I pray you, sirs, be in charity with me, for I am in charity with you."

But Margery was only met with silence. She tried again, in deep humility, "Forgive me if I have annoyed you along the way. And if any of you have in any way trespassed against me, God forgive you for it, as I do." Still fed up, the pilgrims wouldn't speak to her.

Day and night, the ship coursed southward, then cut east through the Greek archipelago. The captain periodically ordered the ship docked at ports along the way to get new provisions: local bread, olive oil, eggs, wine, lemons, and oranges. Time was also needed to fix holes in the hull after the ship had glanced off underwater boulders and to stitch together sails torn by high winds.

The ship raced through the Aegean toward a port just up ahead, as the captain yelled at his crew to drop anchor. The pilgrims clamored off the boat, tired of the smelly darkness, nerves chapped raw. Guy and Gilbert waved back at dark, olive-skinned women heaving themselves out of the windows of brothels dotting the seashore. "Come visit. You can confess afterward next door," joked a raven-haired beauty in Greek to gales of laughter from the other women crowding the windowsill. Uncomprehending, all Guy and Gilbert could do was give silly smiles back.

All along, Margery's yearning to get to the Holy Land increased because ships generally were not allowed to have the Eucharist on board. Seawater could turn it moldy, or a heave-ho of a wave could knock the Holy Bread overboard, a dangerous omen. So, to pass time, Margery listened to holy stories from other pilgrims and prayed.

One morning, Margery awoke and looked around. She was alone. She climbed up the ladder and saw that the pilgrims were already on deck, looking east out to sea, staring at a shimmering mirage that appeared like a white dove feathering her nest. "The Holy Land," bellowed the watchman from the roost as sailors scrambled up the rigging.

The Promised Land. Jerusalem. Nazareth. Bethlehem. City of Jesus, city of apostles, city of angels. The pilgrims exploded in rejoicing. Special hymns were offered up, and the ship's lutes, drums, and tambourines burst forth with songs of ecstatic joy, as Margery melted into a pond of tears.

Into Jaffa they sailed, one of the oldest ports in the world, first inhabited around 7500 BC. It was a surprisingly small city. Margery looked up at the cracked walls and dusty, pocked towers looming overhead, victims of the Crusades, and then down at the warm terracotta rooftops with pots of odd, alien flowers on their doorsteps. Just stepping foot into Jaffa could erase years of sin.

From the shore she looked a little way out into the ocean. Up out of an ancient seabed rose an outcropping where Perseus had rescued Andromeda, a huge boulder Jesus perhaps had looked at when he first called Peter the Rock of the Church. Jaffa was the city where St. Peter began his career as a fisherman, a city where he later performed his own miracles after Jesus died, including raising his handmaiden, Tabitha, from the dead.

The pilgrims collected their belongings and moved onto the dock. Having seen the ship's telltale sails from afar, local wives and daughters roused their husbands and sons from midday naps. Along with city officials, they hurried to the dock on foot, or on camels or donkeys. Ambitious Persians spied on them and everything else they could in the city, peeking around corners.

The Saracens stood on shore staring at these awkwardly obvious pilgrims, waiting for the pilgrims to turn their little town once again into a Christian lunatic asylum. Their wives came up behind, giggling at this comic opera of soggy Christians in their drab clothes with their earnest, righteous manner, wondering at a faith complicated by three warring popes founded by a humble Galilean and the Desert Rose who begat him.

Grandparents arrived, too, comforting crying grandchildren that these damp, pasty-white beings were not drowned dead ghosts from the sea, wondering, too, at what cargo of oddities these cross worshipers brought from the North. Pilgrims searching for salvation, but who would find no deliverance from each other.

Tents were pitched, the official business of welcoming the pilgrims became the order of the day, as olive-skinned men rushed around in long white robes and turbans. Gilbert had already hit a local food stand to gobble down eggs. "You have fried egg on your cloak," Guy scolded him as they stood in line to check in.

"No, that's my family crest," Gilbert said.

"From where, Shite Creek Estates? Wipe it off, you idiot," Guy ordered, as a local priest scowled.

"May the Order of the Fried Egg please come to order," Gilbert said.

Standing on solid ground, Margery breathed deeply. The air was sultry, hot. Even horned adders and snakes sat swelling in the shade behind rocks to cool off. Greeting the pilgrims was the head of the Franciscan monastery, the Prior of Mount Zion, a thin, beleaguered cleric running a Christian outpost in an alien moonscape of a land.

Joining him were the local authorities for the whole entourage, the Mamluk officials from the court of the sultan of Egypt, Al-Mu'ayyad Shaykh.

Guy and Gilbert looked in awe as people they had never seen before walked by, Chinese and African slave traders leading camel caravans, strange priests from mysterious religions that died before Jesus was born. Some glided by in bright, saffron-colored robes wearing midnight-blue velvet caps dotted with silver stars and half-moons atop their heads, looking like priests of Marduk from Numidia.

Christians from ancient sects there in force deeply surprised the English pilgrims. Maronites and Nestorians mingled with Christians from local cultures, Armenians, Greeks, Syrians, and Copts from Egypt.

Margery turned with the other pilgrims to listen to the prior's welcoming lecture, filled with warnings, "The Saracens are quick to exact revenge. Do not get close to the Saracens, and do not quarrel with them. They want the same thing, money."

He cautioned, "Street urchins will pluck at your cloaks, goading you into a quarrel. You cannot fight back, because if you do, that is their license to kill you."

"I'm hungry," muttered Guy.

The friar overheard him and spoke louder, "You are always infidels, apostates to them. Their Qur'an commands them to wage war against you, ambush you, subjugate you, and kill you for the slightest offense, with great reward in heaven. If they capture you, the Saracens will demand money from you. If you cannot pay, they will try to ransom you, and if that fails, they will torture then kill you."

He added, "Don't look at their women. Do not step in their mosques or step on their graves. They see all of that as an affront. If you do any of this, the Saracens will tie your wrists and ankles to pegs in the sand, and they will flay you, then kill you, just as they did one pilgrim a few years ago."

The friar then said quietly, "If they slap or punch you, do nothing, but report it to the emirs. Turn the other cheek is the only way to stay alive. You have left behind your countries for a totally new world. Keep close to your party and do not lag behind. And do not forget our elderly impoverished brethren, the poor monks of Mount Sion in Jerusalem."

"This prior thought of everything," said Gilbert to Guy, who nodded.

The captain and his first mate, as per the pilgrims' contracts, then haggled the fees for their three-day journey to Jerusalem with donkey and camel owners who crowded in.

As they waited, the pilgrims browsed through a bazaar nearby as Bedouin merchants arrived, their camels and bronze horses ferrying goods. The Bedouins unfurled rose-red carpets to sit on and plucked at pulverized orange peels in wooden pots, tossing the fragrant dust on the campfires, scenting the air. Two fanned the flames as they sat around the fire, smoking opium, their camels and horses tethered. They watched the pilgrims as they thoughtfully stroked their ebony brown beards straight, waiting for a sale.

The pilgrims' stomachs flopped as they gazed longingly at bowls of honey in milk, maize cakes baked in even more honey shot through with sticks of cinnamon, dusty floury cakes honeycombed with dates and cardamom, and a type of pancake made of rice pudding, cinnamon, nutmeg, and ginger.

Nearby were bowls of citronade, plum jam, orange marmalade, and brown loaves of sugar. They looked over fat figs, dishes of pomegranates, freshly sliced blood-red oranges they'd never seen before, ripe melons the color of goldenrod, lemons, grapes bruised by the travel, and walnuts and almonds split in two.

For sale, too, were sweetmeats, roasted chickens in coriander, fried eggs, green and dark violet olives. On another blanket sat aniseed licorice, candy of sugared cloves and ginger, and even more spices, different shades of saffron, and a strange red pepper, all laid out in pots on tables. The locals also sold warm wine in little wooden cups with rose leaves.

Servants unfurled carpets of figured dyed cloth from India, waxed linen, muslins, as well as silk carpets from Egypt. Leaves were offered up as mattress stuffing. Plunked down on hemp blankets were blue and pink glass covered boxes, their bottoms made of carved syca-more, as well as hollowed jade and jasper boxes inlaid with ebony carvings. The pilgrims walked past blankets strewn with roped beads of amber, carved peach stones, and cold Orient pearls. They looked at bracelets studded with beryls and chrysolites, at necklaces of green glass and selenites.

Margery closed her eyes in prayer and walked past blankets of even more luxurious, foreign things. Soaps, perfumed ointments to help get rid of the sea stench, tiny cups of perfumes of galbanum, nard, jasmine, myrrh, roses, lilies, and frankincense. All the while, donkeys, camels, and jackals mingled about.

Finally, the pilgrims climbed onto their donkeys as their local guides mounted camels to start on the rocky path toward Jerusalem. Their party quickly joined another group from Germany, which included priests. Now their caravan numbered about ninety in all, along with their captains, tour guides, Franciscan friars, and some local merce-nary soldiers in cinched, white tunics hired as security in the rear.

As the pilgrims started out of town, three boys raced immediately ahead of them and blew through their conch shells, dust clouds curling in the air. More townspeople came barreling out of their homes to stare at the curious, doughy-faced people traveling by.

Gilbert, Guy, and James lowered their heads and tried to sneak sideways glances at the ravishing, exotic women, their eyelids lined with black stibium out to the sides, peering back at them above white chadors. Their husbands glared back at the pilgrims, their airy, long white linen robes lifting in the breeze, revealing a threatening scimitar in the belt of one of them.

A pair of coyotes strolled out from a grotto, walked in circles around the pilgrims, sniffing at the cloak hems of Gilbert and Guy. They inhaled, diffident, then jogged away. "What are they, Jaffa terriers?" Gilbert asked Guy, who shook his head, not knowing.

On the outskirts of Jaffa, as the setting sun glanced off the surrounding hills, James and Gilbert looked back, deeply touched by something they saw from time immemorial, something comforting in the scene unfolding before them.

Just as the townspeople back home did at Lynn's markets, the local merchants broke down their stalls, removed rods from their tents, and folded them. They picked up their stools and blankets and loaded all into woven baskets to scurry back to the warmth of their homes, the locals also part of the inexorable wheel of life moving forward.

The donkeys and camels took to the rocky paths strewn with useless weeds, barren of trees that could have given shade, and gingerly picked their way around lonely boulders. As they walked, the tour guide friar continued to instruct them, "Be meek. Be prudent, and do not smile at them, for they will think you are making fun of them. Keep your faces turned to the ground. Then you will live to see your family again."

Turning in for the night at a hostel in Ramleh, over a meal of watery wine, cheese, and hardboiled eggs, the pilgrims planned the next stage of their journey through the empty, dusty hills of Judea where the apostles had walked with the Lord.

The group remounted their donkeys in the morning. Thieves, who in reality were just little children, jumped out at them from behind trees or large rocks, only to be chased away by the pilgrims' hired Arabian muscle.

They passed empty villages and settlements, dusty and hollow. The Promised Land was spooky and deserted. Bandits ruled the cold desert nights and the lonely stretches between towns. "How can you be a farmer in the desert here?" asked Guy. Looking out at the barren, sandy vistas, Fr. Donald thought, "This is the infertile land still grieving for having accepted Christ's blood. Accursed you are."

As they walked, Margery felt a flood of emotion as she daydreamed about the city that had come to her many times in visions. She prayed, "I beg for your mercy, God, that just as you have brought me safely here to see the city of bliss, grant me the grace to see the city of heaven above." They passed the decrepit ruin that was Jericho and, after a time, finally saw it.

Jerusalem. Some of the pilgrims were so overwhelmed they began to run toward the Holy City. Filled with joy, Margery swooned and fell off her donkey. One of the German priests rushed over to catch her, angry at the English pilgrims. He cradled Margery's head, putting cloves in her mouth to bring her back to her senses. They then took her into their safekeeping. Margery warned the Germans, "Sirs, I beg you, don't be annoyed though I weep deeply in this holy place where our Lord Jesus Christ lived and died."

David's gate rose before them, the entrance to Jerusalem, which Jesus, his mother, Mary Magdalene, and the twelve apostles had passed through. Merely arriving at David's gate won them complete forgiveness of all of their sins, also attainable at all of the shrines in Jerusalem.

Shouting Hosannas and tooting *Te Deums* on their pipes and horns, the pilgrims walked into the Holy City, where every grain of sand, every blade of switchgrass was sacred. The Franciscan friars, who oversaw the holy sites in Jerusalem, took them to the holiest place in all of Christianity, the Church of the Holy Sepulcher, built upon the area where Jesus was tortured, crucified, buried, and rose from the dead, where the angels asked the women weeping at his tomb, "Whom do you seek?"

The caravan headed to a hostel adjoining the Church of the Holy Sepulcher where they would stay for the duration of this leg of the trip. For the first night, they would be locked in the church, as was the custom, keeping vigil from vespers till the next day at evensong.

Upon entering, the tour guide friars lifted up a wooden cross and led the pilgrims singing hymns, each of them holding a wax candle, wavering. They gazed at the remains of the stone pillar where torturers had scourged Jesus. They saw the marble stone Jesus sat on crowned with thorns. Some could swear the purple veins in the slab were spots of blood from Jesus.

They then stepped down to the deepest part of the church, the chapel of St. Helena, mother of Emperor Constantine. Fashioned out of rock, it was here where St. Helena claimed to have discovered the One True Cross during excavations for the church, along with crosses of the two robbers. The pilgrims marveled at the pillars Helena had ordered erected, moist to the touch with water, a miraculous sign that even the marble was still weeping. They hastened back up toward Mount Calvary, more than a dozen feet above street level.

Along with the others, Margery came to where Jesus was nailed to the cross. She looked down at the place where Roman soldiers threw dice and gambled for his robe, where the Blessed Mother wept, where the apostles reeled away in horror, abandoning Jesus, his mother, Mary Magdalene, and John. The pilgrims saw the sacred mound on Calvary where the body of Jesus was laid in his mother's arms after he was taken down from the cross. Some again thought they saw traces of blood.

Margery was suddenly struck with a hyperreal vision of Jesus's crucifixion. Ever since she was a little girl, she had ruminated over Christ's death, grieving over every detail, triggering public sobbing. But here, she could palpably feel the agony of Jesus's pain.

Margery saw Christ hanging right before her eyes, wearing the crown of thorns. Then she suddenly saw a vision of the grieving faces of the Blessed Mother, John, and Mary Magdalene, and the clutch of people who loved Jesus at the foot of the cross.

Suddenly, out came a full-throated, ear-splitting shriek that caused the Saracens sitting nearby to start out of their sandals and the friars to come running, fearing she was being murdered. Margery collapsed to her knees at Mount Calvary, holding her arms up in the shape of a cross. Then she sobbed and writhed on the ground, as a crowd looked on in wonder. Was this epilepsy? No one knew, but what they soon discovered was Margery would no longer be a mystic in a minor key.

Gilbert joked, "I just saw an oak tree jump out of its roots." But Guy was angry, "I wish we had left her out at sea in a bottomless boat." Fr. Donald agreed, "Christ's own mother did not cry as much, nor any saint."

Up ahead lit candles and torches shone at the holiest of all places in Christianity. Here was Christ's tomb aglow inside from torches on the mossy stone walls. When they entered, Margery and the others again plummeted to the ground on their knees crying, beating their chests, their candles toppling over in their hands. Others staggered around as if they were in the throes of death itself.

Guy and Gilbert pocketed pebbles Saracens had secretly strewn on the ground. Others took out burnt pieces of sticks to write passionate messages to Christ or their names near the shrines. Soon, the Saracens had enough of the entertainment. They blew on their conch shells and herded the pilgrims back onto their donkeys to head to the hostel for the night.

The next day the tour guides took the pilgrims along the Via Dolorosa to the hills outside Jerusalem. They went to a Franciscan church on Mount Zion, built near the place where Jesus had washed the apostles' feet, where he celebrated the Last Supper with his friends, and where the Holy Ghost had descended upon the apostles.

All the sites were within a five- to ten-minute walk from each other. Pilate's house. Herod's palace. The house of Caiaphas, the high priest, where Peter heard the cock crow for the third time. The tree where Judas hung himself. The house where Mary cried for joy when her Risen Son walked in the door, where the Blessed Mother gently told Jesus to go see Mary Magdalene crying, looking for him at his tomb.

They scrambled past the Mount of Olives and into the Garden of Gethsemane. Off in the distance was Bethany, where Mary and Martha had run their households, where Lazarus had died and was raised to life by Jesus. Margery was again struck with a vision as she knelt while Mass was being said at the church there. Jesus began talking to her, reminding her that her sins were forgiven a long time ago, "You come here, daughter, not for any need, but for merit, for your sins were forgiven before you came here."

The next morning they traveled to Jesus's birthplace, Bethlehem, about half a dozen miles south, a three-hour trip. Margery was cheerful as she and the pilgrims rode on their donkeys past cypress trees that dotted the way, past sumptuous gardens lining the roads, where fig, olive, and lemon trees grew. A gust of wind felled the almonds among the grapevines, a kind breeze brought the smell of myrtle, touching their sweaty clothes.

The Franciscans ticked off the names of those who had traveled these roads. Abraham with his wife. Jacob, David, Elijah, and

Isaiah. Habakkuk delivering a stew to farmers before the angel of the Lord grabbed him by the hair and carried him off to the lion's den to instead feed Daniel, the prophet, his dinner. "Why was Jesus called Jesus of Nazareth and not Jesus of Bethlehem?" James asked Fr. Donald, who ignored him.

Up ahead were the fields where the Magi saw the star hovering, where the shepherds came running to deliver the news of the miracle that had just happened to the overjoyed visitors hurrying up the hill, that an angel from heaven had announced the Savior of the world was born. The friars told of how the Magi had rejoiced to find other witnesses to this event besides the star that had guided them all those miles, and how they opened their purses to give the poor shepherds gifts for telling them the good news.

Soon, the pilgrims saw the tiny, pauper village of Bethlehem just over a hill, city of the Boy Redeemer where the angels sang peace and goodwill to all men. Margery jumped off her donkey and clapped her hands, a prayer of thanks offered to the sky. In the distance sat the Church of the Nativity, which held the grotto where Christ was born.

First they entered the cave where the Holy Family hid during King Herod's paranoid quest to murder the baby Jesus, where he ordered the killing of scores of baby boys, the first martyrs of the faith. Nearby was a chapel where legend had it the remains of the Holy Innocents were laid to rest. "Why, impious Herod, vainly fear that Christ the Savior cometh here?" a priest quietly sang.

Inside the Church of the Nativity, the pilgrims' eyes adjusted to the dark. Though run down, it was still handsome and imposing, its floor inlaid with mosaic tiling, on top of which stood four dozen marble columns. Nearby was the study chamber of St. Jerome where he had translated the Bible into the Latin Vulgate, where he worked for fifty-five years until he died, his body taken to a tomb in the Church of St. Maria Maggiore in Rome.

The pilgrims entered through a doorway made of burnished marble, and stepped down into a crypt lit by lamps. There they saw the stone slab upon which Jesus was born. Overhead hung a stone inlaid with iron rings to which the ox and the donkey Joseph had brought from Nazareth were tied.

Standing before Jesus's place of birth, Margery again sobbed so riotously that Guy gave a knowing look to Gilbert, who agreed, "No supper with her tonight." So, they banned Margery again. She had to eat with the German friars.

The next morning, the pilgrims headed northeast to the River Jordan, hoping to visit the banks where John the Baptist had baptized Jesus. The road to the river was barren, almost as scary as the Alps. To shake off the growing feeling of dread, Gilbert offered a story about the font of immortality lurking deep in the primordial river. "I heard that if you swim in the river you will come out looking months younger," he said. "If we dunk our clothes in it, our robes will bring us holiness until our dying day, and we can even ward off lightning bolts."

The friars looked at each other. Then one delivered the well-rehearsed, haunting myth of the river to keep the pilgrims in line. "If you jump in the river, you'll be paralyzed and drown," he warned. "If you try to take any water from it, you and everyone with you will be cursed, possibly murdered."

Guy and Gilbert nodded at each other in understanding. "Margery, we have decided you are not to walk with us," said Guy. "Your loud behavior will be too dangerous in this place."

Margery was downcast, but then God told her, "Go with them whether they want you to or not." So Margery did, without their permission, following from behind, as Guy and Gilbert grimaced.

Before them stretched a long, hot, smoldering desert dotted with hills, which they had to cross first to get to the River Jordan. A gust of wind blew the sand, singing a mournful song that things were not quite right here.

Past dusty hillocks they walked, harsh brush and chaparral strewn about. Amid the smothering heat and pared-down dreariness roamed malnourished, ravenous cougars, coyotes, and musty wild hogs. Belligerent nomads looked suspiciously at them over brush top in the distance, as the friars' peripheral vision worked in overdrive to rein in stragglers.

The overdressed pilgrims walked forward into the shimmering landscape, the sun-blasted horizon wavering in the distance. Their woolens itched, the palm leaves under their hats didn't stop the sweat streaming down their faces. They slowly took off layers of clothes down to their linens, as a blazing sun hanging high in the sky threatened to turn them into pillars of salt, like Lot's wife.

"The weather is so hot, I think my feet will burn up," Margery thought. James asked, "Is this the same sun that had looked down upon Jesus?"

The friar leading the way intoned, "Let us pray to our Father in heaven."

As Fr. Donald swatted away at a cloud of gnats, Gilbert said loudly, "I am hungry, let us pray for boiled fish to pop up out of that hot stew of a river."

After passing numerous villages with dry water wells, the pilgrims finally entered the simmering, humid mouth of the River Jordan. In the distance lay an eerie, benighted place where few winds passed over, a calcified place of such desolation and loneliness that, to all who saw it first hand, it was as if they stood on a barren moon of a distant planet. This was the Dead Sea, the bleached out, infertile midriff of the Holy Land. Here ordinary salt was the absolute master, subduing everything, even the scratchy, sawtooth scrub.

Uneasy, the pilgrims continued to walk under the great unrelenting eye of the sun. Hunger pangs gripped their stomachs as they finally sat on the banks of the Jordan to eat. The pilgrims hadn't packed enough food because it would spoil, bringing only dried meat and oily, hard-boiled eggs. They ate glumly, as the friars looked at their ruddy, swollen visages. James and Gilbert dropped back into exhausted slumber.

Meanwhile, Margery lifted her robe, shook off her sandals, and hummed a hymn to herself as she strolled knee deep into the river, past the reeds, daydreaming about Jesus's baptism and how she would have helped Jesus out of the water.

Local Saracens sat on shore about thirty yards away smoking hemp, amused at yet another scene from the theater of the absurd. Intoxicated, they chuckled as they watched Guy and Gilbert delicately walk into the river, reverently cupping the water in their hands to taste it, ignoring the friars' warnings. They roared even harder when the friars raced up and slapped the backs of their heads, "Get out of the water." The pilgrims spat out the warm backwash.

"We are at the arse end of the world and they won't even let us drink here?" Guy said angrily.

"Get your things and get back on your donkeys," the friars yelled. "We are going to the desert where Lucifer tempted Christ, the Man of Men's stomach emptied by forty days of fasting."

The pilgrims then went to Mount Quarentyne where the Son of God battled the greatest tempter of all. They ditched Margery at the base so as to avoid any mishaps. Instead, she got to the top with the help of a Saracen, paying him a groat to carry her up the hill honeycombed with caves, desert hermits popping out to peer at them, then ducking back inside. At the top, yet another Saracen stood, hand outstretched, demanding an entry fee to the chapel.

· · ·

CHAPTER TWENTY-TWO

To Rome

After nearly a month of touring Jerusalem, it was time to head back to Venice, and then on to Rome. There a large treasure trove of earthly holiness, spread over some forty churches, waited with accompanying indulgences.

The Eternal City was where you could see the relics of Sts. Peter and Paul, and the remains of countless other saints, the Coliseum nearby, scented through with the ghosts of Christian martyrs. Rome touted the stairs from Pontius Pilate's praetorium ascended by Jesus during his trial. It had Veronica's veil on which Jesus's face was imprinted, as well as the index finger with which Thomas touched the rib of the risen Christ. It also had the sponge soaked in vinegar and lifted to Jesus's lips while on the cross.

The pilgrims met in the port of Jaffa, their baskets heavy with relics and souvenirs. Margery's fellow pilgrims were still so annoyed with her carrying on, again they stuck her in the rear of the party. But the friars and Saracen families gave her presents and a fond good-bye, charmed by her faith. She looked at her new rosary beads, which stretched the exact length of Jesus's tomb, and her splinter from Moses's rod.

Little rowboats ferried them from the dock to their ship, now patched with cedar wood and sporting a new, capacious bonnet, tanned camel hide stitched together. Once on board, the pilgrims relaxed, no longer fearful of being imprisoned or flayed in the Holy Land.

Within days, however, the hold turned into a miserable ward for invalids, the pilgrims vomiting, their bodies exhausted from the rotten food and the heat. "Fear not, God gave me a message in a vision. No one will die in the ship that I am on," Margery comforted them as they frowned in skepticism.

Pulling into Venice, all were accounted for, no one had died. Margery announced, "We have traveled safely, as God told me we would."

Guy rolled his eyes at Gilbert. "Would you like to come with me to Rome?" Margery asked Gilbert.

"I would not go with you for a hundred pounds," he replied.

With that, they ditched Margery. But Jesus comforted her in a vision, "I shall provide for you very well, and bring you in safety to Rome and home again to England without any disgrace to your body." But under one perilous condition. "Be clad in white clothes," Jesus instructed her. Margery had stopped wearing white after the pilgrims had cut her white robe short. She bargained, "If you bring me to Rome in safety, I shall wear white clothes for your love, even though all the world will wonder at me." But Jesus warned her, "Do not mistrust me."

Right at that point, Margery looked to the side of the road and saw a poor man resting U-shaped on the ground due to an enormous hump on his back, his eyes half shut as he was about to nap. He seemed about sixty years old. "Good man, what's wrong with your back?" she asked.

"It was broken in an illness, ma'am," replied Richard the Irishman, embarrassed, trying to smooth out the multitude of patches on his clothes. Into her mind rose a prophecy from her confessor Fr. Spryngolde long ago, "A poor man with a broken back will come to you after your fellowship has rejected you."

Margery smiled deeply and said to him, "Good Richard, guide me to Rome, and you shall be rewarded for your labor."

"No, ma'am," he answered. "I know very well that your countrymen have abandoned you, and it would be difficult for me to escort you. Your fellow countrymen have both bows and arrows with which they can defend you and themselves, and I have no weapon, except a cloak full of patches."

But Margery set his concern aside, "Richard, don't be afraid, God will look after both of us very well, and I shall give you two nobles for your trouble."

With that, Richard got to his feet. They would first head past Ravenna, Rimini, and Pesaro on the coast of Italy before they cut southwest across to Assisi and then Rome. Soon after came Margery's lectures on upright living. Then the wailing, then her worries her visions were not from God. Richard grew doubtful about his choice to accompany her as he led her along a mountain pass, holding onto the side branches sticking out of the stones.

"Nothing interests me in this world either, except what is of the soul," Richard said after a long talk of heaven, to get on common ground as pebbles made their way skittish.

"By God's grace and upon my soul," Margery began, but Richard interrupted, his distilled, vinegary Irish nature poking through.

"Margery, we have something else in our skulls, not just our souls," Richard said curtly. "It is where your words come from. If you don't listen to how your mouth runs away from you, you will only annoy your fellowship. You won't have joy in life."

But Margery had started singing a church song. Richard elbowed in with a new tack. "Your thoughts are the key notes to your soul," he started.

Uncomprehending, Margery said, "All by Jesus's grace."

Richard sighed.

Finally, they made it to Assisi in Italy, home of St. Francis and his church, which held the cloth Mary had swaddled Jesus with when he was born, so the legend went. Margery prayed over it for forgiveness for all her enemies, friends, and all the souls in purgatory. It was Lammas Day, August 1, a powerful day for the forgiveness of sins. This was the feast of St. Peter in Chains, when Peter was freed from prison by an angel during the night before his trial.

In the church Margery met a woman who would become one of her greatest allies, Dame Margaret Florentine, a wealthy lady from Rome seeking plenary remission. Outside stood her splendid carriage and retinue of servants, horses, and the Knights of Rhodes, a Catholic order of soldiers, as well as numerous gentlewomen. Richard saw an opportunity. He begged Dame Margaret to let them travel with her party to Rome, and Dame Florentine graciously agreed.

The party arrived in Rome in late August 1414. The riverbed of the Tiber footed this riotous, free-flowing city partly built on a necropolis. Sprinkled throughout were ancient ruins and statues, suffused with atmospherics of another time and place. The weight of history was everywhere, an accrual of centuries, leaving them feeling heady.

They walked past slums that were wholly unlike the paintings of Rome back home, which showed children playing in fruit trees with deer roaming in groves. Finally they arrived at the hospital of St. Thomas of Canterbury, the inn for pilgrims from England on the river Tiber. As she walked in the door, the very same pilgrims who had ditched her in Venice looked up in shock. "Protected only by that humpbacked Irish bog rat?" Gilbert asked Guy.

Then Margery irked them even more. Because she had made it untouched to Rome, she bought a white robe from a local tailor, just as Jesus commanded her to do.

In the Eternal City, things got progressively worse for Margery, as she fell into full communication with heaven virtually around the clock. While at church, she had a vision that John the Evangelist heard her confession, as few local confessors spoke English. She had found only a German confessor, Fr. Wenslawe. He suddenly claimed he understood English, though the pilgrims doubted he comprehended a word Margery said. Fr. Donald was pleased when Fr. Wenslawe forced Margery to wear black clothes again.

Then there was an astounding vision soon after in the Lateran, the official seat of the pope and one of Rome's major basilicas. Margery never had a church service to ordain her as a nun, so instead, she envisioned it. She entered into spiritual union with God, the entire heavenly host present. "I take you Margery, for my wedded wife, for fairer, for fouler, for richer, for poorer, provided that you are humble and meek in doing what I command you to do," God said to her.

Afterward, as she walked sobbing across a field toward the inn, a local friar taunted her, "Goat, desist with your bleating," as other pilgrims laughed at her.

As he walked across the field, Fr. Donald mocked her, "I am glad you go about in black clothes as you used to. You shouldn't wear white. There are others holier than you who don't wear white."

But Margery chastised him, "Sir, our Lord would not be displeased though I wore white clothes, for he wills that I do so."

He blew up, "Now I know you are possessed by the devil."

But Margery replied, "If I had a devil in me, I should be angry with you, you know. I don't think I am at all angry with you for anything that you can do to me." Jesus came again to her mind, "I should be crucified anew in you by sharp words, for you shall be slain in no other way."

Fr. Donald then ordered her thrown out of the inn, and Fr. Wenslawe instructed Margery to live with a local poor woman full-time in penance.

Margery grew skinny as a rail, barely eating, wearing a yoke with buckets to carry water for the old lady, gathering sticks to make fires to chase away the notorious, vaporous damp of Rome. At night, there was no bed, only the dirty ground to lie on. No blanket, only her own cloak to lay across her body. One morning, Margery awakened and sat up scratching her head, her hair stiff as pony fur, a kingdom of lice.

Despite all this, her love for Jesus was hitting new heights. So much so that when she came across women in Rome carrying baby boys in their arms, Margery would ask, "Is he male?" If so, she would sob as if she had seen the infant Jesus. All along the streets of Rome, Margery grasped at baby boys as mothers frantically held them close to their chests and scurried away.

Then something else happened. Her ears began ringing with a new sound not of this dimension, obliterating whole conversations. At first it sounded like a pair of fireplace bellows blowing in her ear, then a dove, then a robin redbreast. Then she saw tiny angels flying around, small as dust motes.

Soon Christmas arrived, and Margery donned her white mantle again. "I was ordered to do so by God. My penance is over," she told the German priest, who finally gave in.

Margery quit working for the poor woman, but the pilgrims still wouldn't let her back in, so she lived on the streets. Richard the humpbacked Irishman got into a fight with Margery because she had given away to the poor the money he had lent her, money he had begged for day and night.

Margery stood meekly before Richard as he blasted her, "That was the only money I have in this world. How am I ever going to get that money from you now?"

Margery waited until he was calm, "Richard, by the grace of God, we shall come home to England very well. And you shall come to me in Bristol in Whitsun week, and there shall I pay you well."

Richard stalked away from their table in the inn. "Please remember me in your prayers, Richard," she said to his back. Margery now was utterly alone. She needed to beg to survive. But her negative reputation preceded her wherever she went, which meant she even failed at begging. The people of Rome were afraid she might be a heretic, or worse, of the devil, or at minimum, just a profoundly annoying eccentric, no more interesting than an old cloak.

Fence-post thin, Margery wandered up the Via del Corso, Rome's main road, and into the Church of St. Marcello. She looked up at the unusually lifelike crucifix hanging over the altar, and exhausted, laid down on the cold church tiles to listen for Jesus. Finally, after a time, Jesus came to her, but this time he wasn't encouraging.

"Daughter, you are not yet as poor as I was when I hung naked on the cross," Jesus told her. "You have clothes on your body and I had none. And you have advised other people to be poor for my sake, and therefore you must follow your own advice."

A sob spilled forth. Jesus took pity, "Do not be afraid, for money will come to you." Soothed, Margery walked out of the church doors and into the blinding sunlight. She let the sun adjust her eyes and wandered the streets once more. Ridicule was a trite inconvenience compared to what she suffered now.

After giving away money she got from begging to women poorer than she, Margery wandered into town searching for some bond of human warmth. She blended in with a crowd of beggars outside a church, mansions nearby hugging their pride. Jesus again came to her rescue. Eyes downcast, Margery almost missed seeing one of the first friends she had made when she initially came to Italy.

Looking up, Margery saw Dame Florentine, accompanied by the Knights of Rhodes. She said tremulously, as she simultaneously dropped her face toward the ground, "Dame Margaret." The elegant woman turned around but didn't recognize anyone. When Margery looked up full into her eyes, Dame Margaret's jaw fell open. The lady asked incredulous, in broken English, "Margery in poverte?"

"Yea, grand poverty, Madam," Margery answered.

The lady took Margery into her home for tea and ordered her to eat with her every Sunday, giving her a hamper with food and fragrant wine, as well as money. Seeing the support she received from Dame Margaret, the people of Rome also fed Margery, even asking her to be godmother to their children.

When the brothers of the hospice St. Thomas the Martyr heard about her growing reputation, they caught up with Margery on the street and brought her back in. The pilgrims relented and the status quo set in, for a time.

Soon after, Margery visited the local home of her heroine, St. Bridget of Sweden, on October 7, 1414, the same day the saint was canonized back in 1391. She was thrilled to speak to the saint's own landlord and maiden. Margery stood praying in the bedchamber St. Bridget had died in some forty years before, now a chapel. Once again, Margery's public esteem was restored. But her martyrdom by gossip was just beginning.

• • •

CHAPTER TWENTY-THREE

Home to England

*S*pring 1415 was in full swing. The fields of Rome were sprouting a hesitant green, a perfect time to travel home. Margery had met a new band of pilgrims in Rome, and everything seemed auspicious. They mapped out the trip back to England. Timing was of the essence, for the pilgrims would retrace their way again through the chilly Alps, hoping their itinerary was tight enough so that the wintry snows would be melting.

Tears flowing, Margery said good-bye to Dame Margaret, the old poor woman she lived with, the beggars of Rome, and her German confessor Fr. Wenslawe, who hardly understood a thing she said, just enough to be worried.

Equipped with enough Italian phrases to get them to the Swiss Alps, they set out for England. It had been two years since Margery had seen her fourteen children and her dutiful husband John. She had faced dangers head on. Now her newfound social status in England was ahead of her: pilgrim to the Holy Land, Rome, and Venice. The group walked north for weeks.

They crossed the Alps and passed the city of Constance, where the international gathering of the church elite was still debating. By May, Margery left Europe behind and landed in England. She stepped off the boat, sunk to her knees, and kissed the ground.

While Margery was still in Rome planning the trip home, John was awakened by an early morning light at his bedroom window. He got up from the right side of the bed, went downstairs and sat at the kitchen table, the children still sleeping. Two years earlier, Margery had left him not knowing what to do. The day prior, out of the blue, John had finally confided in Eleanor, William's wife, "I am afraid Margery has been raped or is dead in a ditch."

Touched by John's loneliness, she said simply, "We are here for you."

Later, John found old poems he had read to Margery when they were courting. Reading them made him feel old as a century. They were memories locked in time. He was growing tired listening to the sound of his own voice, tired of wondering when Margery would be coming home.

"Ask me, Margery," he had said to her years before as they walked to Tuesday market.

"Ask you what," she said.

"Ask me why our friends always ask so many questions about you," he said.

"Why?" Margery wondered, worried the gossip grinders in town were again attacking her for self-important airs.

"I said to them, 'why do you always ask me about Margery?' And Catherine and Eleanor said, 'because we love the look on your face when you talk about her,'" he answered, as Margery blushed and looked away.

John looked down at the gold wedding band on his finger and thought of the years gone by, an accrual of sadness. He had no place to go. So instead he wrote Margery a letter he would place in a drawer and never send.

"Margery, a sailor down on the docks showed me a copy of a new thing. It's called the Gough map, he said it's a picture of all of

England's roads and rivers stretching all the way to Bristol and to Northumbria. I said it was lacking, that it didn't show the bridges that we know. Then he got mad at me, went on about some strange words like meridians and compasses. But as I watched him talk, all I could think about was you."

"I miss you even when you're here. Please come home. I am sorry I cannot return to you what I took so long ago, what has given you grief about being impure. What I couldn't tell you then, because I was ashamed you wouldn't believe me, is that Jesus will not stop loving you until he loves you into heaven."

"You would laugh if you could see me now, all loneliness, yes, I know, of my own making. But please know this."

"There is no key that can unlock, no map or bridge that can take me to any other place on this earth that I'd rather be than in the kindness of your eyes."

"Wherever I am, I hear you. Even if you are on the other end of the earth, my heart hears you. That breeze you just felt in your hair is me."

"And know this, too. As you give thanks to your Beloved, please know I am always grateful that Jesus let you go from his arms up in heaven so I can wrap you down here on earth in mine."

As Margery and the pilgrims walked, all things familiar flooded into view, the reel of their journey played in reverse. Spontaneous bursts of song spilled forth from their lips, and Margery stopped her lectures for now, looking forward to seeing her family. She didn't have any money, but that didn't matter. She was on safe ground now.

Margery regaled the traveling party with morality tales, so much so they rewarded her with a few halfpennies, so perhaps she could show John she really was good with money. Or use the funds to repay Richard, the humpbacked man. Even better, the halfpennies went toward candles at Holy Trinity church in Norwich.

As the group moved on, Margery stayed behind in Norwich for a few days to see one of her favorite supporters, the Benedictine monk Thomas Brakleye, an anchorite who lived in the Chapel in the Fields. Early on he had reassured her that her visions were true and holy.

But the other pilgrims and Fr. Donald had already come home loaded with rumors about her controversial behavior, including the hideous tale that Margery had become pregnant on pilgrimage.

Margery waited outside Fr. Brakleye's cell, in line, distracted. Finally, she went in to meet with him.

"Margery," Fr. Brakleye welcomed her coldly. She could see deep concern in his eyes. They sat down in his cell, and he ran his fingers through his hair soft and feathery white like a prophet. He came right to the point.

"How is your new baby?" he asked as Margery looked back at him, upset.

"The baby you begot and bore while you were overseas," Fr. Brakleye continued, churlish. "Is that what took you so long to come home?"

Margery had confronted more powerful dangers. But this was the old rumor that left her dumbstruck with grief. "God knows I never did anything since I went abroad through which I should have a child," she replied, struggling to stay congenial.

Still Fr. Brakleye did not believe her, so Margery tried to go one better, "Sir, I believe the proof I have kept chaste is the trust I have in you that you will give me leave to wear white clothes again."

But to him, Margery only wanted to restore her reputation. Instead he answered sharply, "God forbid it. You just want everyone to be amazed at you."

Margery replied as evenly as she could, "Sir, I don't care, so long as God is pleased with it."

Fr. Brakleye, though, wasn't finished, "Instead, put yourself under my spiritual direction and under a good priest, that is all I can do for you now."

She ostensibly gave in to him, "I will do what God speaks to me." But Margery then had a vision in which Jesus told her, "I do not wish that you should be governed by him." She relayed Jesus's instructions back to the anchorite, his eyebrows raised.

Word had reached the Kempe household in Bishop's Lynn that Margery was back in town, and John raced to Norwich to see her. Riding into town, he saw a woman in white. "Margery," he beamed, running up to her. Margery smiled warmly.

"John, I have missed you so," she said, hugging him.

"Margery, how is your health? The children, they are all good," John began, words spilling out of his mouth, then suddenly glancing at her belly, remembering the rumors. She gave him one look, and he knew not to believe the lies.

Along the way home, Margery told John about her adventures, how Christ rallied to her side, of her new visions firing on all senses now. "Have you kept up your religious observances?" she inquired.

"Best I could, but we have been very short on money," John answered.

They made it home to Bishop's Lynn. The children ran to see her. Margery settled back in, and even though the house felt small to her, the children made it all better. They tightly pulled her legs to their chests, climbed up her hips, and smothered her with kisses. Catherine and Eleanor stopped by, and Margery regaled them, too, with her astounding stories of pilgrimage.

But within days Margery fell seriously ill. Life as a pilgrim had exposed her to overcrowded berths filled with animals, fleas, lice, and fetid air. Though fasting had likely saved her from food-borne illnesses, Margery was weak, her defenses down. As soon as she relaxed, the disease she had been carrying inside broke out and nearly killed her.

Margery lay in bed for days, beset by fever, sweating through her clothes and bed linens. John was frantic, and the children fell sullen, the older ones in a panic. William, Eleanor, Catherine, and Thomas brought food. Priests were called to anoint her with last rites, her eyes, lips, ears, arms, legs, and heart touched by holy oil, the terrifying finality of this consecration feeling like a death sentence. But Jesus comforted her, "You will not die yet."

Slowly she healed, and by the fall, Margery was walking, weakly, her face drained white as a sliced potato. Sunk deep into debt, the Kempe household could not pay its bills. Winter came, and tundra blasts of cold from the North Sea ripped through Margery's home, bringing icy snow and rain. The warmer climates of Italy and the Holy Land felt far away now.

Margery stood in her home, arms wrapped around her, freezing. The family didn't have enough money to buy wood or turf from the fens for heating and cooking. The only warmth came from cheap cresset lamps, bowls with wicks floating in liquid wax.

Despite the difficulties, Margery went to Mass at St. Margaret's church still dressed in white. When the priest spoke of Jesus's passion, she shattered the silence with the new shriek she had added to her repertoire in Jerusalem. Margery sobbed loudly and fell on the ground, writhing. The parishioners jumped in their seats. Years had gone by, yet Bishop's Lynn was still on edge. While she was away, the crackdown on Lollardy had intensified. Mass had been a welcome respite, a quiet, contemplative time.

As Margery walked home, a townsman spat on her and jeered, "You have the Black Death. It is here again; it is making you mad. You howl like a dog."

Walking by, Guy joined in, "You carry an evil thing in you. Go back out to sea so God can take care of you once and for all, you cursed, blasted woman."

Margery replied, "Your torments and malice will only redound to my greater glory in heaven. Indeed, Christ demands it of his followers that they be persecuted for love of him."

Despite the ridicule, Margery's pilgrimage and visions had elevated her to the status of town oracle, a hyper-lucid seer whose prophesies were taken as Gospel truth. But as neighbors pressed Margery for her thoughts on everything, from future harvests to whether their dead spouses were destined for hell, she soon insulted them.

Margery became emboldened to think she could even predict the salvation and damnation of people in her parish, at times with an utter lack of tact. Widows arriving for her prophecies were aghast to hear their family members were stuck in purgatory or going straight to hell. "God will be very pleased if I never cross your threshold again," Margery had truculently told one rich widow enraged to hear her husband was not in heaven yet. Another widow tossed Margery from her home, "Leave at once." Upon hearing her prophesying, Fr. Donald blew up, "Why not just look to Margery for intercession to the Mercy Seat?"

Soon, the people of Bishop's Lynn had enough of Margery. For about a decade and a half she had disrupted their lives and they had patiently taken it in stride. But now they were at their limit. She faced another cold winter of public opinion.

Margery returned to an old idea. She planned a trip to the shrine of the apostle St. James the Greater in Santiago de Compostela in Galicia, northern Spain, a pilgrimage nearly as important as one to Jerusalem or Rome. But the Kempes were strapped for cash, and she needed funds to travel.

Margery asked her friends, "May I borrow some money? I am poor and we owe much debt."

But Catherine chided her, "You are a sieve with money. You'll just as soon give it away."

Eleanor agreed, "You gave away that poor beggar Richard's money. How can we know we'll get our money back?"

Margery said meekly, "Our Lord God will help, for he never failed me in any country and therefore I trust in him."

It took months to finally raise money from supporters, Catherine and Eleanor finally relenting. Winter eased in to spring. Margery packed her things, including a leather purse for provisions. She put on a thrush-grey, fur-lined hooded robe, bought with forty pence from a friend.

It was hard leaving her family. Margery tried to say good-bye to John and the children, but they were bereft. John hung his head and the children cried. They had missed their mother dearly, and now she was leaving again.

That July, Margery embarked on her journey to Spain. But she was met with a huge surprise when she arrived in Bristol to catch a ship. Margery looked up startled to see Richard the Irishman marching toward her, demanding his money back. This time she had the funds to repay him.

Margery was briefly detained after a rich man in her pilgrim party complained about Margery's lecturing to the bishop of Worcester, Thomas Peverel, in town for a visit. A few years prior he had helped send the Lollard John Badby to the stake. As she walked into a church hall for an interrogation, she vehemently crossed herself when she saw the bishop's men in lavish clothes. "What the devil is wrong with you, waving your arms around like you just walked through a spider web," scoffed a cleric across the hall.

"Whose men are you?" she retorted.

"The Bishop's men," they replied sharply.

"No, truly, you are more like the devil's men, given your corrupt clothing," she blasted back.

They exploded with rage. "Damn you, woman," they cursed her. "How dare you, heretic. Who are you to lecture us? Shut up and be quiet."

But they fell silent when the bishop walked in. Peverel had known Margery's father. He had begun his religious career at the Carmelite friary in Lynn in 1377. Briefly questioning her, Bishop Peverel let Margery go, giving her money and asking her to pray for him, for he was sick and old.

After a week at sea, Margery made it to the shrine to St. James the Greater, joining pilgrims from all over Europe. Compostela was a barren, atavistic place. St. James had lived here after the Holy Ghost had descended on the apostles at Pentecost. When St. James went home to Jerusalem and was martyred, his disciples brought his body back to Spain, burying him inside a cave on the mountain. After his grave was discovered, the site became a tourist attraction.

Margery knelt on the hillside, holding up her arms in a cross. She stayed about two weeks. Though it took a week to get there, it took less than that to return to England. Again the pilgrims stared in awe at Margery, believing she had magical power over the sea and sky. That respect would soon be replaced by something more ominous.

CHAPTER TWENTY-FOUR

· · ·

Arrested

$\mathcal{B}$ack in England, Margery and her fellow pilgrims went first to see a famous relic in Gloucestershire, the "Holy Blood of Hailes," supposedly a vial of Christ's own blood at the Cistercian Abbey, even though it was rumored to be the blood of a drake.

The small band then stopped in Leicester, a Lancastrian stronghold. King Henry IV had owned the local castle, and his son King Henry V had held a Parliament there in 1414 to focus on the suppression of Lollardy. Henry V's mother, Mary De Bohun, was also buried there at a local church.

Leicester was a nerve center of religious dissent dating back to the 1380s. Lollards routinely met in the defunct leper hospital of St. John the Baptist on the outskirts of town, run by the heretic William Smith. Lollard scriveners ran a secret factory in town that mass-produced tracts and booklets. Meanwhile, a local Lollard, John Belgrave, busied himself pestering Leicester authorities by regularly nailing tracts and demands to the doors of St. Martin's church, which mocked church leaders.

Entering All Hallows Church on High Cross Street in the center of town, Margery spotted a crucifix, heaven's message of solidarity with suffering earth. She dropped to the ground in a rip-roaring devotional convulsion, alarming onlookers. Margery came to and headed for the church door. A man took her by the sleeve and said sarcastically, "Woman, why are you weeping so bitterly?"

She replied. "Sir, it is not to be told to you." He then hurried along to report her outlandish behavior to town officials.

Back at the inn, Margery asked her new friend, Thomas Marchale, to send a note to her husband to come get her. She was anxious about the mood in the town, and didn't want to go another foot without John. But it was too late.

While Marchale was penning the letter, the innkeeper raced into Margery's room, grabbed her bags, and ordered, "The mayor of Leicester demands your presence," as she quailed. Margery faced her fiercest crucible yet.

As she hurried along outside, a friar with avaricious eyes under a hooded forehead was telling the mayor in his office, "This woman from Lynn is a lying she-devil."

John Ernesby, the mayor, sat back, scowling. A grasping bureaucrat, tall and razor thin, he had a knack for granting his admirers permission to think highly of themselves only if they thought highly of him. "She speaks of visions but she summons them at will," his chief aide added, who had been spying on Margery.

The mayor stood up as if addressing Parliament, even though it was only the three of them sitting there. "Lollards will bring our beloved country to wrack and ruin," he said. "Go drag that tittering imbecile here if you must by the back of her hair."

Margery would be quite a catch to curry favor with the court, as well as seal the mayor's reputation as an avid defender of the faith. Meanwhile, Margery fretted over how to sway the mayor. No scriptural verse was in her bag, only a splinter of Moses's Rod, the relic she got in Jerusalem.

The broad, pasty face of the mayor's chief aide suddenly became alert when he ran into Margery walking in the door. To his irritation, she didn't beg for mercy. Margery instead stood silent, praying. Worse, even the members of the mayor's coterie grew visibly impressed with her spirituality. The mayor and his aides conferred as they let Margery wait outside.

"I can smell Lollards from a mile away," the friar said.

After peering his head out the door to stare at Margery, he looked back and said, "Even if the hand of God reached down from heaven, he couldn't raise these seditionists beyond the depths of their depredations."

However, a monk who had just walked in feared Margery was a saint. "The spy you sent out as a serving boy reported no such evil doing at her inn," he said. "This is a religious matter. The church can punish Margery by making her stand barefoot in her bed sheet at the door of All Hallows on eight Sundays."

But the mayor was ready to take on the mayor's daughter. "No, she'll revel in it," he said. "Call her in."

The friar escorted Margery in to stand in front of the mayor. "Margery Kempe, you now have the honor of addressing the most gifted representative of our fair town and the shires beyond, the mayor," he said, wiping his nose.

The mayor looked her up and down and finally asked, "What town are you from? Whose daughter are you?"

Margery proudly unspooled her bona fides. "Sir, I am from Lynn in Norfolk, the daughter of a good man of the same Lynn, who has been five times mayor of that worshipful borough," she said. "I have a good man, also a burgess of the said town Lynn, for my husband."

Unimpressed, the mayor curled his lips in contempt, "St. Catherine told of what kindred she came, and yet you are not alike. For you are a false strumpet, a false Lollard, and a false deceiver of the people, and therefore I shall have you thrown in prison."

With an iron resolve, Margery replied, "I am as ready, sir, to go to prison for God's love as you are ready to go to church."

However, no one dared speak to the mayor like that, ever, much less a woman. Turning to the friar, the mayor hissed, "As slippery as a French cardinal."

The friar agreed, "And as argumentative as an Italian one."

The mayor stood back up and said, "In your ignorant tittle-tattle, you have openly demonstrated you are a Lollard. I shall burn you at once. Throw her in prison."

Margery blanched. She would have to sit in a common prison in the guildhall until the court of the earl of Leicester was in session. The deputy steward in charge would oversee her inquiry, a menacing, priapic Minotaur of a knight named William who detested Lollards.

Margery was now panicked that she would be raped in prison. She tremulously asked the mayor, "I beg you, sir, not to put me among men so that I may keep my chastity."

The jailer, though, was compassionate. He convinced the mayor to let him lock her in a room in his own house. A few days later, he brought Margery to the hearing, as a crowd grew in number, for she was growing famous.

To prove she was a know-it-all Lollard who had unlawfully read and lectured about the Bible, the deputy steward first tried to trick Margery by speaking in Latin, hoping to tempt the heretic out into the open. In order for a secular woman to criminally read the Gospel, she had to know Latin. The knight sneered, "*Sunt falsa, a praedicatore.*"

But Margery replied, "Speak English, if you please, for I do not understand what you are saying."

The knight let out an exasperated sigh and translated, "You lie most falsely, in plain English." The deputy steward then hit her with a barrage of questions, whether she preached the Gospel, whether she handed out scriptural texts. "How do you know your visions are not from Lucifer?" he demanded.

Margery did not answer, perhaps seeing a trap. Exasperated, the deputy steward would break Margery in another way. "Take her to my private chambers," he ordered.

The door slammed shut, he moved toward Margery, saying lecherous things to her while undoing the laces of his pants. Margery broke down in tears, "Sir, for the reverence of almighty God spare me, for I am a man's wife."

Thwarted, the knight pulled up his pants. He threatened, "You shall tell me whether you get this talk from God or from the devil, or else you shall go to prison."

Margery answered meekly, wiping away tears, "Sir, I am not afraid to go to prison for my Lord's love, who suffered much more for my love than I may for his. I pray you, do as you think best."

Finally, the deputy steward gave in. "Either you are a truly good woman or else a truly wicked woman," he said as he called for the jailer to set her free.

"This is a church matter," the deputy steward told the mayor and his men, the responsibility of the abbot of Leicester, Richard Rothley, a church stalwart. Besides, lightning storms had just rocked the town, raising fears Margery's arrest had brought them on.

Margery was to be put on ecclesiastical trial in All Hallows Church. The abbot of St. Mary's and the dean of Leicester would sit on the tribunal, along with friars, and priests. On the day of her trial, Mayor Ernesby hustled into the church along with the locals and Ruth and Mathilda, who suddenly arrived.

A friar stood up on the tribunal and called the crowd to silence. He walked forward, took Margery by the hand, and brought her to stand before the abbot and his assessors. "Put your hand on the Bible and swear that you will answer truthfully about your beliefs," the friar ordered. The crowd bent forward.

The clergymen then fired questions at Margery about the articles of the Catholic faith. Any mistake could lead her to a stake the mayor was already erecting in his fevered brain. "Margery Kempe of Bishop's Lynn, do you or do you not believe that the bread and wine at Holy Mass becomes transformed in the priest's hands into Christ's flesh and blood?" the abbot demanded.

Margery replied, "Whatever man has taken the order of priesthood, be he never so wicked a man in his manner of life, if he duly says those words over the bread that our Lord Jesus Christ said when he celebrated the Last Supper sitting among his disciples, I believe that it is his very flesh and blood, and not material bread."

But Margery had exposed an opening, a potential leaning toward Lollardy. The Lollards had questioned whether the Holy Eucharist was invalid if a priest was in a state of mortal sin. Instead, correct intent, *ex opere operato*, was enough to make the sacrament valid.

The sharpest among them stood up and said, "Did we just hear an eloquent case for capital punishment? What point of law are you trying to make, Margery, quote 'be he never so wicked a man in his manner of life'? Must a priest be of irreproachable character or not for the Eucharist to be valid?"

"No, I reject that idea," Margery contradicted herself, showing she was familiar with the controversy. "Once he is ordained a priest, even if he is evil, at that instant of the Eucharist he has been given the divine order from God to be the vehicle of his miracles."

A senior monk with a face like a catfish who supported her said, "Margery answered right well doctrinally, as all priests are sinners to a degree. Orthodoxy, not heresy is present here."

But Mayor Ernesby grew enraged she was getting away with her equivocation. "This woman is hip-deep in heresy. Many a Lollard has shrewdly used such neat sophistries, only to relapse into heresies," the mayor loudly told the gathering. "Truly, she does not mean with her heart what she says with her mouth."

Her judges consulted. The mayor's reputation was on the line. Margery trembled, her face pointed to the ground, her hands clasped in prayer, shaking like aspen leaves. Moments ticked by. A friar pulled on the mayor's sleeve. "She has a weak spot with which we can stop her," he whispered.

"What is that?" the mayor hissed back, irked.

"Sitting in the heart of a heretic is always self-doubt," he replied. "Find it and we will win."

The mayor smiled, loudly cleared his throat, and said, "Margery is a strumpet full of demons deceiving you even now."

The clerics broke from their huddle. Then came the mayor's coup de grace, "She has slept with many men on pilgrimage," as the crowd gasped.

It was a notably acute charge. Margery was accused not just of the black sin of adultery, but of luring pilgrim husbands away from their wives. She had so angered everyone that this charge alone could send her to the stake. She looked at the vivid scar on her hand, only Margery knew what she had endured.

The abbot forcefully asked the mayor, "Your proof?"

A smile spanning his face, the mayor answered, looking at Margery to see if her nerves were cracking, "Why else was she gone all this time but for this foul reason, so her pregnancies would bear fruit so we would not know the better of it?"

"Demoniac," a spectator hissed at Margery.

A man just to the right of her chimed in, "We should cut you up in little pieces and feed you to snakes." Margery visibly trembled, but she still looked stoically ahead and waited for the gathering to fall silent. Then she spoke. But Margery didn't buckle.

Instead, the molecules of her body rearranged back into Bishop's Lynn's most powerful daughter. With preternatural calm, Margery coolly replied, "Sir, I take witness of my Lord Jesus Christ, whose body is here present in the sacrament of the altar," as the mayor nervously shifted at the last part, "that I never had part of any man's body in this world in actual deed by way of sin, except my husband's body, to whom I am bound by the law of matrimony and by whom I have borne fourteen children."

Sitting in their pew, Ruth muttered to Mathilda, "Talk of commoning in church, leave it to Margery."

As the crowd fell silent, Margery said, "For I would have you know, sir, that there is no man in this world that I love so much as God, for I love him above all things, and sir, I tell you truly, I love all men in God and for God."

Then suddenly Margery turned on her heels and looked directly into the eyes of the mayor. The crowd braced, increasingly anxious that Leicester was run by a maniac.

"Sir, you are not worthy to be a mayor," Margery said firmly in the same stentorian voice she had inherited from her father. "And that I shall prove by Holy Writ, for our Lord God said himself before he would take vengeance on the cities, 'I shall come down and see,' and yet he knew all things. That was for nothing else, sir, but to show men such as you are that you should not carry out punishments unless you have prior knowledge that they are appropriate."

As the crowd's murmuring picked up, Margery ended her thunderclap of a speech, "And sir, you have done quite the contrary to me today, for, sir, you have caused me much shame for something that I am not guilty of. I pray God forgive you it."

The senior monk said, "My God, we all know of the recent storms that have beset our town. Is Margery vowing even worse weather?"

Put back on his heels, the mayor rounded about. He saw the crowd was turning on him, faces of irked disbelief that this vindictive man almost had them burn alive an innocent woman, possibly a saint, inviting death and destruction on Leicester. His mind boiling, still his deepest motivation was to beat Margery. The mayor reached for the final arrow in his quiver and aimed it right at the chauvinists in the crowd.

The mayor shot back, "I want to know why you go about in white clothes, for I believe you have come here to lure away our wives from us and lead them off with you."

But Margery adroitly batted him away, "Sir, you shall not learn from my mouth why I go about in white clothes, you are not worthy to know it."

As the mayor's eyes shot daggers at her, Margery coolly added, "But sir, I will tell it to these worthy clerks by way of confession. Let them consider whether they will tell it to you."

The mayor was dumbfounded. Margery had deftly removed the test of her orthodoxy out of his hands and put it back where it belonged, in the hands of the church. The abbot turned on the mayor and ordered him, "Go away from us, all of you. We must hear what Margery has to say about the secret of her white mantle."

Once the crowd had been pushed outside and the doors slammed shut, Margery knelt on the ground and spoke. "Our Lord by revelation ordered me to wear white before I went to Jerusalem," she confided. "And so I have told my confessors. And therefore they have charged me that I should go about dressed like this, for they dare not go against my feelings for fear of God."

So even the most powerful men in England shouldn't stop it. "Therefore, sirs, if the mayor wants to know why I go about in white, you may say, if you please, that my confessors order me to do so, and then you will tell no lies, yet he will not know the truth," she advised.

The clerics went back into a huddle. "Margery has proven herself not a follower of Lollardy, but of church," the senior monk advised the abbot.

The abbot agreed, "Even if God told her to wear a robe made of seagrass and pussy willows, she would. But what to do about the mayor?"

"Fool, he has always stomped around like an old castrated ape," the senior monk replied. "More importantly, Margery has given us a legal out."

They called back in the mayor. "This is a religious matter. Her confessors here and in Rome approved her white clothes, and she is bound to their obedience," the abbot summarily told the mayor. The mayor was stunned, struck through with a wounded defensiveness. Margery walked out of the hall. The crowd slowly erupted in cheers.

Margery had won, a woman who had interrupted many a Mass, a married English housewife with fourteen children who paraded around in virginal white lecturing about the Gospels and scolding the clergy. Fearing his loss of power, but not ready for rapprochement, the mayor turned a sour face to Margery hoping a public show of reconciliation would clear his name.

But he hissed, "I will not let you go from here in spite of anything you can say, unless you go to my lord Bishop of Lincoln for a letter, inasmuch you are in his jurisdiction, so that I may be discharged of responsibility for you."

Margery, however, was already acquainted with Philip Repingdon. She replied, still trembling slightly being near this man, "Sir, I certainly dare speak to my lord of Lincoln, for I have been very kindly received by him before." But some in the crowd were surprised the two enemies were talking.

A worried onlooker asked, "Are you all right Margery? Are you in charity with the mayor?"

Margery replied, "Yes, and with all whom God has created."

Then she turned back to her tormentor and said, "I pray you, be in charity with me. Forgive me for displeasing you."

The mayor answered, "All is well now, Margery." Perhaps hoping to rethread their tattered relationship, he ventured, "Margery, you should write a book." She didn't answer, but hurried away.

Margery got a letter from the abbot certifying her orthodoxy, along with a written record of her trial to bring to Bishop Repingdon. Meanwhile, her friend Thomas Marchale was waiting at a hostel in Melton Mowbray, panicked his friend had been martyred. He stopped people out on the street. "Has Margery been burnt?" he demanded. Hearing she won, he sent his friend Patrick to help escort Margery out of Leicester.

Margery then set off with Patrick on horseback out of Leicester. "If you come again, we'll treat you better than before," a crowd of backers regaled her at the city gates.

But just a little way outside of town, Margery discovered she had left behind her bag with her cherished relic of the rod of Moses and asked Patrick to retrieve it. The intemperate mayor, though, arrested Patrick and interrogated him about Margery, "She's a liar, how many men has she lain with?" When Patrick couldn't say—he hardly knew Margery—the mayor finally let him go but kept her bag and relic.

Sullen, Margery then traveled to see Bishop Repingdon. He greeted her warmly and then immediately shot a note back to the mayor admonishing him to stop pestering Margery. "And send back her purse at once," he ordered.

Finally, the mayor sent her bag back but made Margery wait three weeks for it. Still trying to get home from her pilgrimage to Compostela, Margery took a detour to York with Patrick to visit the shrine of St. William, the Archbishop of York supposedly killed by drinking poison in his chalice in 1154. Miracles were reported to occur at his tomb in the York Minster.

Here Margery was in her element. She sat talking freely of the Gospels in the Minster, heady surroundings for its roots dated back to the seventh century. A priest who disliked Margery sidled up and asked, "How long will you stay here, woman?"

"Sir, I intend to stay for fourteen days," Margery replied. She then turned back to her new friends, talking at length of her pilgrimage. The people sat listening in rapt attention, as authorities grew angrier by the minute. Margery then disrupted their Masses. "Jesus I die for you. I die. I die. I die. Jesus, mercy," she yelled.

Margery was now a town nuisance who had overstayed her welcome, the situation was growing combustible by the day. Curiosity seekers from the farmlands were piling into town just to see the crying lady, laughing and pointing fingers at their overlords.

Town officials met in the office of the mayor of York. "Margery Kempe is turning us into the biggest fools in Christendom," a senior aide said ruefully.

A friar said melodramatically, raising an index finger to the ceiling, "She will befoul forever the name of York and ruin us and you, mayor. We must send this Lynn quack back across the Ouse River."

"But how can we? We have no standing," a monk said. They sat thinking. Suddenly, they had an idea.

The law at the time said all wives must carry a certificate, a sort of medieval passport, showing that their husbands permitted them to travel unchaperoned. But few women carried these documents, and authorities hardly ever enforced the law. The monk felt the move against Margery was wrong. "It's unfair. Even a snake is honest enough to attack in the face. Why the subterfuge?" he demanded.

The friar retorted, "Because we must not get trapped in the thickets of her words." So they sent a summoner slithering Margery's way. He caught up with Margery on the street as she was speaking to a small gathering. "Woman," he said unctuously. "You said when you first came here that you would stay only fourteen days?"

Margery first looked at him with love, but she decided to be obtuse. "Yes, sir, with your leave, I said that I would stay here fourteen days, but I did not say that I should neither stay here more nor less," she replied. "But now, sir, I tell you truly that I am not leaving yet."

He drew himself up to his full height and announced, "Then I order you to appear two weeks from today at a hearing in York."

Margery gasped, "I shall obey your order with a good will." Another hearing. Margery was tired. Again she needed to rally people to her cause, to show her judges she had good churchgoers on her side, supporters now dwindling.

Margery turned to her new friends, important members of the York episcopate: Master John Aclom, a doctor of divinity, Sir John Kendale, a canon of the minster, and another man who was a vicar choral at the Minster. Aclom vowed to endorse her after Margery begged him, but the vicar choral balked until he knew which way her case was heading. Frustrated, Margery grew afraid.

The day of the hearing dawned grey and cloudy. The chapter house was packed with a crowd of the curious, her detractors, followers, and friends from home, Catherine, Eleanor, and William. John had to stay behind to take care of the children with Thomas. "Be cheerful, Margery," they encouraged her. But then the friends stared angrily as Gilbert, Mathilda, Guy, and Ruth walked in hoping for entertainment.

Margery stood in the center of the hearing room. She looked up and inwardly breathed a sigh of relief. There sitting next to the judges was her friend, John Aclom. The bar was also packed with clerics and doctors of divinity who were inclined to look kindly on her. But her chief inquisitor stepped forward and opened the hearing brutally quick.

"Woman, what are you doing here in this part of the country?" he asked.

Margery replied, "Sir, I come on pilgrimage to offer here at St. William's shrine."

He asked sarcastically, "Do you have a husband?" knowing full well she did.

"Yes," she answered.

As Margery was answering, he swiftly moved to a table loaded with documents and held one up as an example. "Do you have a letter recording his permission, to let you travel about alone?" he demanded.

Flustered, Margery clearly didn't have the paperwork. "Sir, my husband gave me permission with his own mouth," she replied, as laughter rippled through the clerics. Now she was in serious trouble. But Margery wasn't having any of this folderol.

"Why do you proceed in this way with me more than you do with other pilgrims who are here and who have no letter any more than I have?" she demanded. "Sir, them you let go in peace and quiet and undisturbed, and yet I may not be left alone amongst you."

Increasingly agitated, Margery sallied forth, "And sir, if there be any cleric here amongst you all who can prove that I have said any word otherwise than I ought to do, I am ready to put it right very willingly. I will maintain neither error nor heresy, for it is my will entirely to hold as Holy Church holds, and fully to please God."

"What a magnificently prideful woman Margery is," a cleric said to a monk seated behind him, as he stood up to take her on. He hit Margery with a barrage of questions about the articles of the faith, the seven works of mercy, the seven gifts of the Holy Ghost, and the efficacy of the seven sacraments.

Margery answered truthfully as she could, but the judges were not satisfied, "We order you to defend yourself at a hearing before the Archbishop of York at Cawood."

Henry Bowet, the Archbishop of York, was a commanding, bull-necked man, the second most powerful leader of the Catholic Church in England and a lifelong personal friend and confidante of King

Henry IV and his family. He had followed Henry Bolingbroke into exile, and had supported Bolingbroke's overthrow of the king.

Bowet was held in such high esteem, he was later treasurer to the king, who also entrusted him to deliver his important letters to the pope. The monarchy had also given Bowet the difficult See of York, his predecessor, Richard Scrope, beheaded for leading a northern rebellion against King Henry IV, an execution that shocked the country.

Margery was brought to the local chapel in Cawood to stand trial. As clerics and priests strolled into the courtyard, they mocked her.

"Damned Lollard," one cursed her. "By God Almighty, we look forward to seeing you burn."

Despite the fact Margery faced the stake, she rebuked them, "Sirs, I fear you will be burned in hell without end, unless you correct yourselves of your swearing of oaths, for you do not keep the commandments of God."

But the crowd grew hushed as a retinue of powerful senior clerics walked in. Right behind them strolled the Archbishop of York, the formidable Bowet. He had already gained infamy across the country for his brutal interrogations of heretics, his men nearly beating to death the suspected Lollard, William Cooke.

Jesus came to reassure Margery in a vision, "Everything will go well." As the archbishop took his seat, she knelt before him. But Archbishop Bowet startled Margery by brusquely getting right to the point, "Why do you go about in white clothes? Are you a virgin?"

Margery said, "No, sir, I am no virgin. I am a married woman—"

He abruptly cut her off, "You are a false heretic. Guards, get the fetters, arrest her."

Frantic, Margery said in her defense, "I am no heretic, nor shall you prove me one," words that faded away in the tumult.

The archbishop left Margery standing alone while guards marched forward and again slapped metal cuffs on her wrists. The archbishop returned moments later with more officials. She ignored their entrance, lost in an inner discussion with God. "Help me, dear Lord, protect me against all my enemies," she prayed. Then Margery broke down in tears.

In all her previous trials, heaven's fanfare of a martyr's welcome had warmed her heart. Burning, beheading, or disemboweling were martyrdom in the abstract as celestial trumpets sounded. But now the white-blue flames were physically nearer, as was the excruciating pain. Loudly weeping, a seizure suddenly struck Margery and she collapsed, convulsing violently before the archbishop and his stunned coterie.

"Jesus I die for love of you. I die, Jesus, mercy. Oh, Jesus, I am so sorry," she wailed. "St. Peter, St. Catherine, and St. Bridget, I love you. Come help me."

Astonished, a priest remarked, "We have never seen such crying."

Though shocked, Archbishop Bowet was touched, partly because he heard Margery invoke St. Bridget. He was a learned student of this saint, held in great esteem in the Lancastrian court. Margery came to, sat up, but then fell back down again on her side. Still all business, the archbishop asked, "Why do you weep so, woman?"

To Margery, the archbishop had thrown down a gauntlet. Challenged, she chose not the way of the meek. Margery stood up before the archbishop and looked him right in the eye. "Sir, you shall wish some day that you had wept as sorely as I," she said stoutly, as the crowd clucked at her impudence.

A friar asked loudly, "Didn't St. Bridget also publicly chastise the king of Sweden, Magnus Erikson, for erring in his Christianity?"

Undaunted, the archbishop thought, "I'll flush out the heretic." So he, too, drilled Margery on the articles of the Catholic faith. As he bore down, Archbishop Bowet suddenly sprung on Margery a trap.

"What of the belief that, if you were to look at the Eucharist, that it would be just the same as looking at a wooden statue of Jesus or Mary?" he asked.

But Margery answered without hesitation, "The real, corporal presence of Christ is there."

His clerics took mincing steps backward as he whirled on them, "She knows her faith well enough. What shall I do with her?"

They shouted back, "We know very well that she knows the articles of the faith, but we will not allow her to dwell among us." Another warned, "She might lead the people astray."

The archbishop turned back to Margery. "I am told very bad things about you. I heard it said that you are a very wicked woman," he said.

Margery didn't take kindly to being called wicked by a jumped up, pretender knight in a miter's cap who gave religious orders only after he stuck up a wet finger in the wind of popular opinion. She barreled beyond the point of no return.

"Sir, I also hear it said that you are a wicked man," she retorted, as the gathering gasped. "And if you are as wicked as people say you will never get to heaven unless you amend while you are here."

Archbishop Bowet growled, "Why, you, what do people say about me?"

She answered curtly, "Other people, sir, can tell you well enough."

A senior cleric in a fur-lined hood stood up and said, "Quiet, you speak of yourself and let him be."

But the archbishop held his temper. He could lose both his credibility and his people by burning a popular woman. Seeing the gears of his mind working, a long-faced senior cleric whispered, "It would be dangerous steering upstream against public opinion if you choose to condemn this mother. Tack your sails to the wind, calibrate indignation to the people's love for her. Do not overreact."

But the friar who despised Margery hissed, "No, you are wrong, she must be brought to heel. The mayor of Leicester failed."

The senior cleric laughed, "That mayor had no more sense than a mollusk. Should we suffer the same public humiliation as the mayor, who almost witlessly started a riot? Do not treat this pickerel of a woman as an enemy of the state, as if the church is a besieged encampment. Stridency will make you appear weak. Overreact like a powerless, aggrieved minority, and you will become one."

As Bowet sat back, the cleric continued, "St. Bridget was God's fiddle, Hildegard of Bingen his trumpet. Margery is just his fireplace bellows. Turning the other cheek is power. A lion does not roar at mayflies. A mighty archbishop does not launch military campaigns against English mothers."

Bowet said, "A compelling battle plan."

The senior cleric had another idea, "Perhaps Margery can be our banner in towns where we cannot be. Just as Oldcastle and Wyclif sent Lollards into the hinterlands, let us be happy to slipstream behind her. Let others years from now grow old and fat debating all the pots and kettles clattering about Margery, whether she is a heretic, saint, or neither."

The archbishop smiled, and turned to Margery, "You shall swear that you will not teach people or call them to account in my diocese."

But she replied, "No sir, I will not swear, for I shall speak of God and rebuke those who swear great oaths wherever I go, until such time that the pope and Holy Church have ordained that nobody shall be so bold as to speak of God. For God Almighty does not forbid, sir, that we should speak of him."

An electric charge vibrated through the clerics. Now, finally, Margery was caught. "What do you mean, 'God Almighty forbids not that we shall speak of him'?" the friar demanded.

Margery blithely barreled forth, "The Gospel according to Luke said our Lord told a woman, 'In truth, so are they blessed who hear the word of God and keep it.' And therefore, sir, I think that the Gospel gives me leave to speak of God."

A priest chortled, "Here we know that she has a devil in her for she speaks of the Gospel."

The friar said angrily, "You just cited the same Gospel passage the Lollard heretic Walter Brut used arguing for women's right to preach: 'Even more blessed are those who preach and keep it, because it is more blessed to give than to receive.'"

Amid explosive shouting, Margery whirled about in circles, looking from cleric to cleric. The friar argued to the archbishop, "Your grace, Margery Kempe is lying to you. She just proved her Lollardy because she clearly has studied the Bible. She is preaching, and that is against the law."

Another friar read aloud from a Bible St. Paul's approbation, "No woman should preach."

Visibly shaken, Margery said loudly, "I do not preach, sir, I do not go into any pulpit. I use only conversation and good words, and that I will do while I live."

But now she was perched on a high wire. The archbishop was cornered. He had no choice but to send Margery to the flames.

CHAPTER TWENTY-FIVE

Fighting for Her Life

As Archbishop Bowet deliberated, the cleric who had already examined Margery in York opened a new line of attack.

"Sir, she told me the worst tale about priests that I ever heard, proving she is a heretic," he said.

"Repeat these terrible stories, Margery," Archbishop Bowet ordered.

As carefully as she could, Margery told a fable in her defense that she had overheard years ago as a teenager, having to do with, of all things, a brown bear, a story that again would deliver the priests a thumping. The assembled clerics leaned forward expectantly, as Margery spoke of a priest who got lost in a forest. When night came, he fell asleep in a garden, which had a pear tree in the middle abloom with flowers. Then came a great bear who shook the tree, knocked down the flowers, and greedily devoured them.

Margery lowered her voice in all Christian rectitude, "And when he had eaten them, turning his tail towards the priest, he discharged them out again at his rear end." Roars of laughter startled Margery, and her white gable hood fell down her forehead. She fixed her hood, stood up straighter, and continued.

"The priest, greatly revolted at that disgusting sight and becoming very depressed for fear of what it might mean, wandered off on his way all gloomy and pensive," she said loudly, as the laughter subsided. "He met a handsome old pilgrim and asked him, 'What does this mean?'"

The hall fell silent, the clerics intrigued. "The pilgrim, showing himself to be the messenger of God, thus addressed him, 'Priest, you are yourself the pear tree, flowering when you say Mass and administer the sacraments, although you act without devotion. For you take very little heed how you say your matins and your service, so long as it is babbled to an end."

As the clerics looked at each other, astounded, Margery raised her voice, "You receive there the fruit of everlasting life, the sacrament of the altar, in a very feeble frame of mind. All day long afterwards, you spend your time amiss, buying, and selling, bartering and exchanging, just like a man of the world. You sit over your beer, giving yourself up to gluttony and excess, to the lust of your body through lechery and impurity. You break the commandments of God through swearing, lying, detraction, and backbiting gossip, and the practice of other such sins."

Then she finished it off, "Just like the loathsome bear, you devour and destroy the flowers and blossoms of virtuous living to your own endless damnation and to the hindrance of many other people, unless you have grace for repentance and amending."

Shocked, the churchmen looked at each other, then to Archbishop Bowet. Margery's survival hung by the thin thread of his already taxed forbearance.

But the archbishop surprised them all by finally saying, "An excellent story," for he was genuinely amused by Margery's audacity. "She speaks the truth. We all can name flippant priests who gobble through the Eucharist just to quickly race off to alehouses, to barter deceitfully, have sex, hunt, hawk, and drink all night, only to roll into church the next morning still tanked up with ale to snore through Mass or doze over their rosaries."

Bowet declared, "No heresy here. Margery is only saying that she supports good priests and the right order of the church. She bows to my jurisdiction and to church authority."

But still Margery needed to be gotten rid of. "Where shall I find a man who might take this woman away from me so she'll stop disturbing the peace?" the archbishop asked his men.

Soon, a man named John from the archbishop's own household was hired for five shillings to take Margery out of town. She piped up gaily, annoying the archbishop, "Our Lord shall reward you very well for it."

Irked, he ordered John, "Lead her fast out of this county."

But then she was arrested again. On the way back to Bishop's Lynn the next day, the friars whom Margery had enraged convinced the yeomen of the Duke of Bedford to arrest Margery as an aide to Oldcastle. Now she once again stood trembling on trial in Beverley before the Archbishop of York.

"Woman, what do you say to all this? Speak up, what do you have to say in your defense?" the archbishop demanded.

"My Lord, saving your reverence, all the words that they say are lies," Margery replied, looking at her accusers.

The crowd waited, anticipating the worst. His trusted senior cleric whispered in Archbishop Bowet's ear, "Your grace, if Margery Kempe truly is the consort of that devil traitor, Sir Oldcastle, and the female leader of the Lollards, ask yourself this: Didn't Oldcastle escape us for years by hiding? Why then would Margery conspicuously parade around the countryside dressed in white?"

The archbishop looked at him as the cleric added, "Don't be Margery's Magnus Erikson."

Finally, the archbishop announced, "You all relay falsely, translating what your wicked hearts hear into slander against this woman.

Friar, the words are not heresy, they are slanderous words and erroneous."

But Fr. Donald was enraged. He was the Dominican friar who suddenly had arrived to announce he was the one who had tried to send Margery to the stake in Bishop's Lynn for criminally preaching the Gospel, that her visions and sobbings were done for show. The archbishop's decision now meant his reputation was on the line. Fr. Donald bit back, "Protest she may, but the Duke of Bedford will have her head on a pike."

As he spoke, Margery had plunged to her knees swaying. The crowd looked up at the archbishop, dozens of pairs of beseeching eyes.

"Well, friar, and you shall escort her to him," the archbishop ordered Fr. Donald, a shrewd move. He bellowed over the uproar, "For I find Margery innocent of all charges. Her words are not heresy."

Fr. Donald panicked, "No, sir, it is not a friar's job to escort a woman about."

The archbishop retorted, "And I will not have it that the Duke of Bedford be angry with me because of her."

He turned to his men and said, "Take this friar and watch him until I examine him again, and take Margery, too. I need to examine her further." The tribunal was ordered to spend another day mulling the matter. Margery was led back to a local inn for the night. Irked, Fr. Donald went to a nearby parish house.

The next morning, as Margery walked in, a church cleric ordered her to meet with the archbishop in his bed chambers. Margery had to defend herself to a man in his bedroom. She walked in and knelt by his bedside.

"I thank you, gracious lord, you are an upright and just..." Margery began, but the old man waved his hand as if batting off a bothersome gnat.

"Yes, yes, I am told worse things of you than I ever was before," the archbishop said peevishly.

Margery grew worried, "My lord, if you care to examine me, I shall avow the truth, and if I be found guilty, I will be obedient to your correction."

But that might not be good enough, because the archbishop had just heard a lethal charge against her. He sent his chief steward into the church hall to summon a powerful cleric, John Rickinghall, confessor to the Duke of Bedford, the same Rickinghall called in by Henry Le Despenser to oversee Sawtrey's renouncement of his Lollard beliefs.

"Now, sir, as you said to me when she was not present, say now while she is present," the archbishop ordered.

"Meddling in dynastic politics, breaking up a royal household, all treasonous, which will lead to death," Rickinghall said as he glared at Margery, who looked back, stunned.

Margery was now charged with leading away the royal ladies of the court from their husbands, tantamount to treason. To protect the bloodstained borders with Scotland, the monarchy desperately needed the chain of powerful alliances between the nobles with their lands and militias in the north, the Greystokes and the Westmorlands. If their wives ditched their husbands, chaos would ensue, the wall would be breached, jeopardizing the kingdom's first line of defense against the Scots.

"Woman, you were at my Lady Westmorland's," Rickinghall said.

"When, sir?" Margery demanded.

"At Easter," he shot back.

The senior monk standing there came to Margery's defense and snapped at him, "What of it? Margery only speaks of our faith and the Fisher of Men."

Rickinghall replied icily, "Margery Kempe is a widower of men come to seize our wives, fomenting rebellion in a royal household, which is treason. The mayor of Leicester was right. She has come to divide and conquer us by stealing our wives."

The enemy friar said to Fr. Donald as they stood eavesdropping outside the window, "Clever move by Oldcastle, to have a Lollard wife poison royal wives."

The Lady Westmorland Margery had visited was Joan de Beaufort, a powerful royal at court. Joan was the granddaughter of King Edward III and the half-sister of King Henry IV. Beaufort was also aunt to the reigning King Henry V and the Duke of Bedford.

Joan's daughter, Elizabeth was married to John, Lord Greystoke. For some mysterious reason, Elizabeth later refused to be buried next to her husband in his family's plot, and instead was buried in the Dominican friary in York in 1434.

Rickinghall said, "My lady herself was pleased with you and liked your talk, but you advised my Lady Greystroke to leave her husband. Now you have said enough to be burned for."

Margery gasped. She had not seen Lady Westmorland at Easter. She had visited with her a long time ago. She quickly turned to Archbishop Bowet and pleaded, "My Lord, he is wrong. I did not see Lady Westmorland at Easter. I have not seen my Lady Westmorland these two years and more. She sent for me before I went to Jerusalem. If you like, I will go to her again for a testimonial that I prompted no such matter."

The chief steward standing at Bowet's side chortled, "No, we'll get the affidavit ourselves. In the meantime, put Margery in our prison for forty days and you'll see how she'll love God the better for it." But the archbishop was curious, "What exactly did you tell Lady Westmorland?"

Margery hesitated, but then replied, "It was a good tale of a lady because she would not love her enemies, and of a bailiff who was saved because he loved his enemies and forgave them their trespasses."

The archbishop thought for a moment. Again he rescued Margery, "This story isn't about splitting up marriages. This is just a good, simple lesson of Christ's message of forgiveness."

Rickinghall glowered as Margery clapped her hands and looked to the ceiling in relief. The archbishop added, "I believe there was never a woman in England so treated as she is and has been. I do not know what to do with you." Finally, Margery was set free. Looking out the window at the crowd cheering upon hearing the news, the archbishop's chief steward said, "Let her go from here this time, and if she ever comes back again, we will burn her ourselves."

The archbishop finally wanted to be rid of her once and for all. Margery came up with an amicable solution, "My lord, I pray you, let me have your seal as a record that I have vindicated myself against my enemies and that nothing admissible is charged against me, our Lord be thanked. And let me have John, your man, again to bring me over the river Humber, where I will leave your diocese behind and you shall never see me again."

The archbishop sighed in relief at that last part and said, "Yes, on one condition. You must receive certification from the Archbishop of Canterbury that you are an orthodox follower of the faith."

Another high priest to conquer. Archbishop Arundel had died in 1414 and his certification of her orthodoxy was now a worthless parchment. She would have to see the new archbishop, Henry Chichele, a ruthless enforcer and Lollard hunter. Still, she was happy. Margery thanked the archbishop and walked out into the great hall as cheers slowly erupted.

"Pray for us," shouted the members of Archbishop Bowet's household. But her new enemy, Bowet's chief steward, stood watching, still offended. He could not resist one parting shot.

"Holy folk should not laugh," he said.

Margery yelled back smiling, "Sir, I have great cause to laugh, for the more shame and scorn I suffer, the merrier I may be in our Lord Jesus Christ." She walked a few paces, but then stood stock-still.

Outside the doors of the great hall stood her archenemy, Fr. Donald. Seething, he spat out in rug-chewing rage, "You illiterate, evil upstart of a strumpet. You have humiliated the righteous once too many times." But he didn't get far, because Margery hurried away.

. . .

CHAPTER TWENTY-SIX

Banished

*M*argery wanted to head home to Bishop's Lynn to her family, whom she had not seen since leaving for pilgrimage to Compostela. But she first had to fetch her husband so they could go together to see Archbishop Chichele in London.

Margery walked the road back home. She was feeling creaky, feeling old. She had so much to tell, tales of adventure, of thwarting the king's brother, of tweaking the beards of the church powerful.

As she stopped to rest in a monastery in West Lynn, Margery asked some of her supporters to go ahead of her to tell her husband John that she could not come home just yet, but must take a detour to London. Nodding off in a room at the monastery, she awoke a few hours later, rubbed her eyes and looked out the window. "Strange, that figure looks familiar," she thought.

Then a warm smile broke out. It was John. Margery ran out the door, up the road and hugged her loyal husband, the man who had taken care of her fourteen children. John looked into her eyes and grabbed her chin, "What, now dressed in black? You finally washed your white mantle?"

Along the way, she updated John about her trials. "It seems I am not welcome anywhere," she said sadly as they walked along, the October sun brightening autumn leaves turned red and orange. John then talked to her just as he always did, a language that was their mutual level of understanding.

"Margery, your entire life you have been doubted because you make people uncomfortable," he said thoughtfully. She looked up at him, expectant.

"Sort of the same problem for the one you love, the way I see it," John continued, reflective. "Problem for Jesus was, he could see everything. He was the most observant of all. He put himself up there on the cross because he could see right through everyone. And people don't like that, not the Pharisees, not the Sanhedrin, Herod, or Pilate. Pride lies. Humility sees."

They had come to a T-junction in the road, where they could only go right or left. They turned down the road toward London. John continued, "Same for you, Margery. People don't like to be seen for who they are. The truth is, if Jesus walked the earth again, he still would be killed, again and again, because men find guilt intolerable. They can't forgive themselves."

As Margery slowly smiled, John continued, "Yet I think what Jesus wanted us to see is that, he saw, accepted, forgave, but then he moved on. He got the worst death of anyone, ever, but what did he do? Still he forgave, he resurrected himself, got up, and walked away."

Margery offered brightly, "And laughed merrily, too, said Julian."

John smiled and said, "The devil makes you despair that you don't matter. Same for when people feel threatened. They want to make you not matter. But Jesus makes you believe you matter, because you do."

Margery's eyes registered understanding as John finished, "They want to kill you because they think they only see pride. But you already know that Jesus is all humility. That is your salvation, humility."

Maybe this wasn't a marriage where they lived happily ever after, every day. Time had sanded off the edges of their relationship, but it still had emotions that were an echo of their beginnings, and that would suffice.

The journey to London was smooth. The Kempes pulled the bell at Lambeth Palace and were hustled in past walls painted with designs of gold finches, butterflies, bees, flowers, moons, and stars.

Henry Chichele had received the triumphant King Henry V at St. Paul's Cathedral in 1415 after the famous Battle of Agincourt. Now, as England's most powerful religious leader, Chichele fiercely enforced Arundel's laws, even coming up with his own set of interrogatories to root out heretics.

Archbishop Chichele scanned Archbishop Bowet's trial record of Margery, saw that she was orthodox, and after a brief discussion, signed the certificate. With her church passport in hand, Margery and John finally headed back to Bishop's Lynn for a joyful reunion with their family and friends.

Months passed, and their family routines set in. Easter of 1418 was coming, and the Kempes' children ran home with holiday ornaments they made at school, baskets filled with boiled eggs, leaves, and ribbons.

But John had already found the joy of rediscovering his wife was complicated. Margery suffered increasing scorn and slander as she wailed again at St. Margaret's. "Like Chanticleer the rooster," Guy said to Gilbert in the back pew.

Walking out on the road after Mass one day, Gilbert threw a bowl of filthy water on Margery's head from his upstairs window. Master Alan later comforted her, "St. Bridget also had a pail of dirty water dumped on her head, too, by an immoral advisor the saint had told the Swedish King Magnus to cast out."

Margery took it all in stride, "I thank God for this humiliation, too."

Life in Bishop's Lynn went on. But Margery again fell deathly ill, with dysentery, or perhaps a gall bladder attack or appendicitis. Many nights she lay in bed sweating and vomiting into a bucket, her creaturely feelings reinforcing her sense of lowliness.

John raced to call Fr. Spryngolde to again give Margery last rites, as her children wept seeing their mother too weak to lift a spoon. Margery was sick off and on for eight more years until 1426, retching for hours on end, throwing up gall. John didn't know what to do.

"Patience, John, to bear my illness, otherwise I may not endure it," she asked, and he nodded. Finally, Margery got better. But all the while, her public wailing reached new, dramatic heights.

Margery increasingly sobbed and chastised herself before Mass, during Mass, after Mass. Behind her back, the townspeople roared with laughter and children mimicked her.

She cried for up to six hours on Good Fridays, on other days for the sins of the people, souls in purgatory, for those in distress. She wailed for anyone who didn't know Jesus, for false heretics. Crying at a Pieta in Norwich, the statue of Mary holding her dead son, a priest chided her, "Woman, Jesus is long since dead."

Margery whirled on him, "Sir, his death is as fresh to me as if he had died this same day, and so I think it ought to be to you and to all Christian people."

One day, Margery heard at Tuesday market that a famous Franciscan preacher was heading to Bishop's Lynn. William Melton was a dazzling orator. His fierce, eloquent sermons were a popular draw, and people traveled from miles around just to hear him. All gave him the same thing he demanded, undivided attention.

Before he came to town, Margery continued to sob, endangering Lynn's chances at a world-class event. That's why after the friar arrived, both Fr. Spryngolde and Master Alan decided to talk to Margery. They found her sitting alone in a pew in St. Margaret's, lost in reverie. Fr. Spryngolde sat down next to her, Master Alan on the other side. She finally opened her eyes.

"Please, daughter, I beg you, stay silent. Please don't cry when the good friar speaks," Fr. Spryngolde said gently. "Can you do that?"

"Yes, sir," she replied.

Their next stop was Friar Melton's chambers at the Greyfriars Tower just outside town. Fr. Spryngolde began, "Sir, a woman will come to hear your sermon, Margery Kempe, who, when she hears the Passion of our Lord or any high devotion, weeps very loudly. Please bear her patiently."

The friar nodded, as Master Alan added, "It is her vocation. She calls it God's gift to her and to us all."

Fr. Spryngolde had an idea, "Good friar, maybe you could hold off talking of the Passion, for that seems to bring about the most boisterous kind of crying."

The friar replied, "That's a right well idea."

So, Friar Melton took to the pulpit in the Chapel of St. James that Sunday, people standing in the aisles. He avoided the Passion in his homily. Margery smiled back at him for love from her pew. It held for a time, until one day he forgot and mentioned the Lord's scourging.

Margery burst out with a huge sob. Friar Melton quickly wrapped it up. She tried to bottle up her crying inside, but that made her sobbing worse. The friar grew increasingly enraged at her interruptions that clanged like an old church bell, he wanted Margery to go home and be quiet. "I wish this woman were out of the church. She annoys the people," Friar Melton confided to some of the churchgoers after Mass.

Her friend Catherine defended her, "Sir, please excuse her. She can't control it."

Guy broke in, edified that the friar didn't like Margery either, "She has a devil in her."

Folding his arms, the friar threatened, "Well, I won't suffer her to hear my sermons unless she leaves off her sobbing. If she won't stop, I will curse her from the pulpit."

The situation was now a full-blown crisis. Cursing Margery from the pulpit would be tantamount to excommunication. Fr. Spryngolde and Master Alan again hurried to Friar Melton's chambers and tried to persuade him over a bottle of wine. But he was adamant, "If she makes any more noise, I will have no choice but to speak against her from the pulpit."

But then he offered a compromise, "I will let Margery come listen to me on one condition. If she acknowledges that her crying is a sickness, I will have compassion for her and urge the people to pray for her."

That angered Margery. "This is no sickness. I know it by revelation and by experience of its working. I will not for all this world say otherwise," she told the two when they met with her.

Having no choice, they advised, "Then do not go where he preaches." Instead, Margery was tucked away, like a forgotten relic stowed on a shelf, in St. Nicholas Chapel on the other side of town, her sobbing sounding like a very sorry distant hoot owl.

Margery sat in the chapel and loudly cried, staring up at the great multi-colored west window, listening to the perfunctory sermons of priests who came to say Mass just for her and a scattering of local recluses. John stayed at home with the children, sometimes coming to sit a few pews behind her, as was their habit.

This period was one of the saddest Margery had ever known, because attending Mass and listening to sermons were her entire life now. Crestfallen, she walked the streets of Bishop's Lynn, once again utterly alone.

Meanwhile, Friar Melton had ratcheted up his preaching against Margery. The intensity of his attacks reached a boiling point in a sermon in the yard of St. James Chapel on July 25, the Apostle St. James the Greater's feast day. Without naming her, he laid out all of her flaws, citing the good example of Martha and Mary. His sermon left the people of Bishop's Lynn conflicted.

"Well, I won't be attending his sermons any longer," Catherine said to Eleanor.

When Friar Melton got wind that he was being talked about behind his back, he smacked his hand down on the wood of the pulpit the next Sunday and again threatened retaliation against Margery, "If I hear these matters repeated any more, I shall so strike the nail on the head that it shall shame all her supporters."

Worried, William, Eleanor, Catherine, and Thomas arrived at the Kempes' home to give Margery the only way out. "Margery, it is better for you to leave town than stay because so many people are against you," William advised as John and their friends looked at the ground. His words stung. In profound sorrow, Margery looked at them. But then she remembered her mission.

"I shall stay here as long as God wants, for here in this town I have sinned, therefore it is fitting that I suffer sorrow in this town because of it," Margery said. Then she began to reflect, "And yet, I do not have as much sorrow or shame as I have deserved, for I have trespassed against God. I pray God that all manner of wickedness that any man shall say of me in this world may stand towards remission of my sins." She added, "All contempt, shame, and reproof belongs to me."

After her friends left, she went to pray in the Chapel of Our Lady in St. Margaret's Church. "Margery, what will you do now? There can be no more against you but the moon and seven stars," Fr. Spryngolde said as he sat down.

Her voice reedy thin, Margery replied, "Sir, cheer up, for everything will be quite all right in the end."

But then came a startling turn of events, one that worsened Margery's reputation even more. Jesus told her, "Go back into church, for I shall take away from you your crying, that you will no longer cry so loudly."

So, Margery didn't cry as much anymore in church. That's when many in Bishop's Lynn finally turned against her for good. "I always said she could stop her tears at will," said Fr. Donald.

"False hypocrite," Guy replied.

Her martyrdom by gossip worsened. At night, Jesus came to Margery and said, "Now you have the true way to heaven. By this way I came to heaven and all my disciples, for now you will know all the better what sorrow and shame I suffered for your love, and you will have the more compassion when you think on my passion. I have tried you in poverty, and I have chastised you as I would myself, both within your soul and outwardly, through people's slander."

As she turned in for the night, Jesus added, "Daughter, I tell you, truly, the friar shall be chastised sharply. As his name is now, it shall be thrown down and yours shall be raised up."

CHAPTER TWENTY-SEVEN

. . .

Margery's Miracle

*J*ust as Margery had traveled to the outer limits of socially accept-able behavior, she was banished to the outer limits of Bishop's Lynn, marooned as if she was on the dark side of the moon. Margery had felt rejection before, but this time it hurt deeply, a profound spiritual pain.

It was made worse because now the Kempes were living apart to uphold Margery's reputation of chastity, John in a house nearby. The couple agreed that if they tried to live together as husband and wife, the gossips in town would attack Margery for being a false hypocrite, pretending to be virgin chaste.

By now, her children had grown up, grown apart. Her second home, St. Margaret's Church, where she talked to Jesus and he talked back, didn't want her around anymore. Her usually avuncular confessor had made that clear.

Margery's heart ached, worn down by the years of being openly derided as a disturbed fake. The shame of the heresy charges from so many church trials and hearings still stuck stubbornly to her reputa-tion. And throughout, Fr. Donald still turned many against her.

Then when it couldn't get any worse, it did. Jesus and his Mother suddenly ordered Margery in a vision to eat meat again, after years of abstinence. Now Margery was deeply afraid because she knew the backlash would be severe. She couldn't take much more malicious gossip. Jesus advised, "Take no heed of their scorn."

Sure enough, the town shot a cannon blast of rebukes at her stoked with lies. Over dinner soon after Fr. Donald said to Friar Oliver, "What, first Margery can shut off her waterworks at will, and now she is eating meat again? Even in her abstinence she ate the best, most expensive pike, not the sour red herring. She is an eccentric old fool."

On the morning of January 23, 1421, Margery stood up from her wooden bed with the straw mattress in her empty house on an empty byway. She walked hesitantly to St. Margaret's cathedral where she stayed for hours, alone, sitting in a church pew in the back corner. She couldn't stop crying, but this time, out of shame.

The midday sun soon brushed the church's stained-glass windows dusky pink. Outside the men and women were starting to pack up their local shops to hurry home for dinner. Margery thought she heard muffled sounds knocking about, but ignored it. A few minutes later, there was a crash, then a strange acrid odor. Smoke.

"Have they finally come for me?" she asked aloud, panic-stricken.

Instead, a hellish fire was on the march and Bishop's Lynn was on the run. A devastating blaze had burst open in the renowned Trinity Guildhall across from the church and was just now threatening the thatched rooftops all around. Margery's hometown was about to turn into a roaring inferno.

Margery ran outside and watched, stunned, as a burst of flames blew out a window in the guildhall. The fire suddenly split into a blitzkrieg of hundreds of flames that jumped off the guildhall's rooftop and marched on top of the houses nearby. With terrifying, lightning speed, the flames then leapt onto the roof of the stately home of Geoffrey Cantley, a town leader, as he ran out the front door.

Timber, bricks, and mortar crashed to the ground. Horses reared up and bolted, children howled in panic, and fathers and mothers ran zigzag with their families through the town square, along with terrified cows, pigs, goats, dogs, cats, roosters, and chickens. "The beaters, the beaters!" William shouted as he ran into the square with John Kempe, their friends and family close behind.

With fearsome speed, the bonfire suddenly lurched ninety degrees around and, whipped forward by the wind, took aim right at St. Margaret's, marching across the rooftops toward the church. Sparks and smoke streamed toward the crossing tower of the cathedral. Men pointed and shouted in anguish, and women began to wail.

A glass-covered hole in the church roof, the lantern vault on nicer days usually showered sunlight on top of the heads of parishioners below, delivering a natural halo. But now rivers of flames, fiery sparks, and black smoke were pouring toward the vault threatening to break through. Fr. Donald stood next to Friar Melton as both looked up in shock.

"Here it comes. It's jumping for St. Margaret's, get the buckets," John yelled.

Men, women, children, grandparents, bakers, cobblers, bankers, lawyers, religious recluses, monks, friars, and priests raced chaotically to water wells, canals, to the Ouse River, the North Sea, to any available water in sight. They frantically set up a bucket brigade. Sparks flew like a cloud of lightning bugs all around them, nestling in their hair, stinging their eyes and biting their ears as they desperately passed along buckets. Others tried to beat the flames out with rugs, blankets, and brooms, as blue-black smoke choked their lungs in the dry winter air.

Margery reeled in terror and sobbed loudly, praying to the sky, now a compact vault of smoke and whizzing sparks, "Grace and mercy for the people."

But even Margery's crying was no use. Even with all the water in the North Sea the townspeople couldn't deliver it quickly enough into the square with their pails, soup pots, and leather aprons. It was like trying to put out a raging volcano with teacups of water. The fire continued advancing. "The devil is winning," Fr. Spryngolde said in tears as he raced over to Margery, who was on her knees in front of the church, distraught, arms raised in a cross.

"Margery, get over here. We need you to haul water," Ruth yelled at her.

Margery started to run, but then stopped to look up to heaven again to say another prayer. "Sure, we'll wait for you as the town burns to the ground," Mathilda mocked, as Margery put her hands over her face, humiliated. Catherine shot her an angry look as Eleanor grabbed Margery by the arm and said, "Margery, call upon his Holy Name for a flood."

Margery raced back into St. Margaret's church. Now smoke was cascading into the choir loft through the lantern, the fire was on St. Margaret's doorstep. Distraught, Fr. Spryngolde grabbed her arm and asked, "Margery, ought I take the Holy Eucharist and raise it up before the fire?"

Margery gasped, "Yes sir, yes, for our Lord Jesus Christ told me it will be well."

With Margery close behind, Fr. Spryngolde grabbed the Blessed Host in the monstrance from the altar and held it up in procession out the front doors of St. Margaret's. He pointed it first at the furnace at the guildhall, then swooped around and aimed it at the cathedral, hoping this powerful, heaven-sent talisman would send the flames rocketing back to hell. It didn't work. The fire continued unabated.

Running into the middle of the square, Margery desperately cried out with a loud voice, tears streaming down her face staring at the destruction, "Good Lord, make everything all right and send down some rain or storm that may, through your mercy, quench this fire and ease my heart."

But Fr. Donald yelled from the middle of the crowd, "Cry the Ouse River, Margery," as some roared with laughter. Ashamed, Margery retreated to the side of St. Margaret's, crying. That enraged William.

Moments ticked by. Meanwhile, Margery had knelt on the side of St. Margaret's, her hand on its outer wall.

Then a white flake gently drifted down. Then another, and within minutes a gigantic snowstorm blew in. Suddenly snow was everywhere. Pancake-size snowflakes blew about in a maddening, dizzying pattern, engulfing the town square. The townspeople look at each other, blinking icy flakes out of their eyes. Then they looked at St. Margaret's and swiveled back to the guildhall. Their jaws dropped open.

Somehow, not wet rain, but a calm, velvety blanket of snow, heaven-sent, was now extinguishing the worst fire Bishop's Lynn had seen in decades. Margery had asked God for deliverance for all to plainly hear, and God had answered in the simplest form of miraculous precipitation, snow, heaven's reminder of eternal joy.

Three men covered in white snow grabbed Margery and hugged her, hoisting her up off the ground. They cheered, "Look, Margery, God has shown us great grace and sent us a fair snowstorm to quench the fire with. Be now of good cheer and thank God for it."

Shouts came forth all around as the crowd jigged and danced through new piles of snow, "Thank God for Margery. God save Margery."

Margery beamed. "God told me it would be well, and it is, through a miracle," she said.

William turned to Fr. Donald, who was standing with Friar Melton, and said, "All these years, you have relentlessly made us all think we are not good enough. But every single one of us was born good and to do something special. This is a miracle. We are all miracles, like the people of Bethsaida who brought loaves and fishes were the miracle that day. But somehow, you have blinded yourself to miracles, and tried to make us blind, too."

As Fr. Donald turned around, he suddenly saw the scene unfolding before him wasn't just one of destruction. It was all of Bishop's Lynn having turned out to help. Fr. Donald was now shocked to find the turning of the cosmic wheel had brought his disgrace. Even Friar Melton became a convert to Margery's cause and shunned him.

"Look who's sitting over there," Thomas said as he nodded his head toward the other side of an alehouse in Lynn where they sat still in celebration the next day.

William said loudly, "Margery's ruination is all he has created his entire life."

Catherine said, "Just a sack of platitudes, such a bore."

Stunned at what he overheard, Fr. Donald looked down. He said quietly to the wood of the tabletop, "The pursuit has been more satisfying to me than the end result of my desire. My life is a lesson in hypocrisy." Finally, after all those years, Fr. Donald came home to himself. He got up and went outside to cry in the backyard of the tavern.

Meanwhile, Margery was walking by the front of the tavern. The crowd shouted out the door, "'Tis full merry in here as it is in heaven, Margery. Come join us!"

Catherine said, "That's our Margery, God bless her, sobs and all."

But Margery didn't hear them, her face was bent down deep in prayer. She was heading back to St. Nicholas Chapel on the other side of town. "None of that anymore," said Friar Melton, sending Master Alan to gather her back in to the tavern.

Later, Fr. Donald tended to the wounded, many of whom had third-degree burns on their arms and legs. He stopped Gilbert from ill-advising Mathilda, Ruth, and Guy to paste their burns with butter, which the four of them got trying to save Guy's shop. Ruth sat glaring at her husband because his hoard of animal skins to artificially raise their prices had turned their family business into a charred mess.

"All of you, go stand in the ocean. The salt water will cleanse and close your wounds," Fr. Donald ordered, and they did, and it worked. The cosmos wheeled on its mysterious way.

CHAPTER TWENTY-EIGHT

Passings

*B*ack at their separate homes in Bishop's Lynn, Margery and John were getting old, both in their sixties. They had stayed married for nearly four decades but were still living apart to avoid gossip. Margery was still a commanding, though now fragile woman. John was the same sensitive, quiet, loving man.

Before dawn one morning, John lay in his bed in his house looking out the window, raising his hand to his hair, already thin. He strained his gray-blue eyes, barely seeing the downs outside. Then he thought he heard a sound. Was that Margery crying? Or one of the grandchildren?

John got up barefoot, walked out of his bedroom, and then slipped and crashed down the stairs, hitting the ground floor first with his head. The din awakened their neighbors. Catherine ran to get Margery, who quickly grabbed her sandals from a row of shoes under her bed, dingy, repaired. All came running, their hearts broken to find John lying in a pool of blood, his head canted outward unnaturally, twisted under his arm and shoulder.

Doctor Gunther, much older now, came along with Fr. Donald to plug the five holes in John's head with linens, later returning to stitch them. "There's not enough blood in him to keep a sparrow alive," Fr. Donald warned, as Margery looked back, grave.

John was finally allowed to move back in with Margery. He laid in bed for months on end, his family fearing for his life. Ruth started in again with Guy at their repaired shop at market, "You know, Margery is to blame for this. If John dies, she should be hanged for his death. She has been no good wife."

Guy agreed, "She damn near killed him so many times. It's a wonder he made it this far."

Attack they did, even though it was these same gossips who had kept Margery and John physically apart. But now even Fr. Donald fought them back down into silence, finally feeling the goodness of what it felt to be loyal.

Gradually, John healed, but he was different now. Part of him was gone. He became an infant once more, time and space relative. He couldn't help it, he was incontinent. His life had come full circle.

John spent his days watching Margery light fires to cook for him, spoon-feeding him. Washing out his undergarments was penance for lustful memories of their nights of sex. Margery bathed John's exhausted body, just as gently as if he were the infant Jesus. One day John, who could hardly speak, pointed at Margery's chest, then at the bathtub, and fought to say, "Always good at this, you."

Margery grinned back as she watched him smile with his eyes, and then looked out the window at the evergreens, then further at the stone fences in the distance intersecting the fields leading down toward the shore. Later that day, Margery was getting linens out of a drawer and discovered a yellowing letter John had written decades before.

She called for Catherine to come over to read it to her. They sat on his bed as she read, "Know that Jesus will not stop loving you until he loves you into heaven," and "there is no other place I'd rather be than in the kindness of your eyes." Margery's heart broke. She started to cry.

Margery made a new vow to John to make his remaining years the best she could. She burned fragrant wood to make their home a pine-scented place. As he slept, Margery kept watch over John, smoothed his hair, and pulled his blanket higher. One morning, he opened his eyes and gently smiled at her. As she got up from the chair by his bed to get his breakfast, he grabbed her hand, still marked by the vivid scar and kissed it. Margery turned away, blinking tears.

Then, as the days turned softly into weeks, then months, one day, just as quietly as he had come into this world, John Kempe left the planet to return to the Great Love waiting at the hushed borders of the earth.

John died peacefully in autumn 1431, a few months or so after Joan of Arc was burnt at the stake. It was the same year Margery's beloved son also died, after he had abandoned his wanton ways, became a father, and returned to life as a reformed Christian, finally understanding his mother.

All this time, Margery had yearned to touch the tangible pieces of heaven. But all along her John was a part of that paradise, standing smiling right before her. For all love is divine, is God's will. Margery wept tears of gratitude, then prayed earnestly for her husband's safe passage into heaven.

Now a widow, Margery devoted herself to charity. Back in 1389, her father had led a commission into leper houses on the outskirts of town. Grieving how she had feared and detested lepers as a young girl, Margery worked as hard as she could with the religious at sick houses like the Leperhouse of St. Mary Magdalene, which sat on the outskirts of Bishop's Lynn on the causeway leading to Cawood. Master Alan was a Bible reader there.

Housed there were people with ulcerated noses and ears dropping off in sour liquids, hands and feet fingerless and toeless, restricted from wandering in public. If they did, they had to wear a bell. They also were ordered to attend Mass and were given a herring and a farthing on Maundy Thursday.

"I must kiss them, for I am kissing my Lord and Savior Jesus Christ," she told Fr. Spryngolde, begging permission for this corporal work of mercy. But Fr. Spryngolde instructed, "Kiss female lepers if you must, and no men."

So Margery fell down on her knees before two female lepers at the hospital as they looked up astonished, and told them, "I must kiss you for love of Jesus. Your illness is a blessing, for it means you will be in heaven with our Lord, so long as you cheerfully offer up your sufferings to him."

The two women looked at each other and looked back at Margery. They let her kiss them, as Margery wept. As they watched Margery walking to the leperhouse, Ruth joked to Mathilda, "My husband says it's his French cousin, the ghost of Guy, come to haunt Margery to do penance for the sins of lust she and John committed." Mathilda finally said, "Oh stop it," as Ruth looked up, startled.

By this time, Margery had seen plenty of shrines, annoying her daughter-in-law by demanding she travel with her to Aachen, Germany, so as to see the three Hosts of the Eucharist miraculously stained with the blood of Christ. A group of pilgrims in Germany ditched Margery there, too, her crying too much to handle, calling her the Englishwoman with the tail. Even her German guide gave Margery back the money she had paid him and left her behind.

Back at home, priests looked up to Margery as a mystic from days of yore. The Dominicans would affirm her holiness at an annual meeting. She was asked to help adjudicate a spat brought to the Archbishop of Norwich, William Alnwick, over whether the Chapel of St. Nicholas could have a lucrative baptismal font, too, rejecting it in favor of St. Margaret's.

Archbishop Alnwick would later be an assessor of Joan of Arc at her trial, the Duke of Bedford overseeing Joan's execution behind the scenes. About seven accused heretics were known to be put to death in England in the years leading up to Joan's execution. Archbishop

Alnwick would also oversee the Norwich heresy trials of five dozen Lollards in Margery's hometown area, for saying things like, "A baker makes thirty Eucharistic hosts in one hour, so did he make thirty Jesuses? How can a priest make his creator? Aren't hosts made of bread, so why worship what is man-made?" Many were let go with a penance, but accused heretics and seditionists were executed by the score in ensuing decades.

Friar Melton had his own sudden crying jag in the pulpit, finally understanding Margery. Even her attackers Ruth and Mathilda now begged Margery to come cry for them as they lay dying, their husbands long dead, William, Eleanor, and Thomas gone, too. Margery prayed as Ruth and Mathilda lay trembling, overcome with the sudden manic piety of sinners fearing demons might come to escort them to hell.

All the while, the older she got, the more undeserving Margery felt. She yearned to be with Jesus in heaven so she would no longer displease him. One day she had a striking vision that she was crying with the apostles as they kneeled at the bedside of the dying Blessed Mother. Margery cried so much and so loudly, however, she even annoyed the apostles. "Stop and be quiet," they ordered.

But Margery rebuked them, "You do not want me to cry over the Mother of God dying? I am so full of sorrow, I simply must cry and weep."

As Margery finished washing the pewter dishes at home one day, she looked out of the window into the late afternoon sky, the clouds touched rose gold by a setting sun. It was 1436. All was peaceful, quiet, the world softly turning on its axis as though God stood rolling the earth under his feet, the earth remotely beautiful, a deep azure blue. God stood still on the outside, eternal, God was time. Across town the star watcher Nicholas was still staying up late into the long nights of miracle and wonder, peering deep into the black sky, searching for signs of the Creator Invisible somewhere out in the silence of space.

King Henry IV, his sons King Henry V and the Duke of Bedford, and Thomas Arundel were now dead, Julian of Norwich was gone, too. In a distant place across England, ashes wafted off charred stakes abandoned at Smithfield, just for now. Lonely cinders blew about in a lazy dandelion afternoon, picked up by a breeze that delivered memories down Lynn's byways and out of town to men and women who sat hushed over candlelight talking of the Lollards, of Wyclif, Sawtrey, and Oldcastle, the first but soon-to-be forgotten Christian reformers.

Margery was now an old holy woman, an immutable presence comforting to the people of Bishop's Lynn, the nostalgia of hearth and home. The same things would afflict the soul today as they would tomorrow—jealousy, pettiness, anger, gossip, slander, and malice. Margery's life sacrificed for all of that, yes, her own behavior to blame. But the clarity of her beliefs and her faith in her visions were still fresh and real. Because Margery believed there was better, there was more.

Should she start a religious order, as St. Bridget did? Margery didn't have the money, because money never mattered to her. Yet she still wanted to tell others about Jesus. Margery looked at the yellowing attestation of the Archbishop of Canterbury's wax seal peeling off her old certification. She remembered how Bishop Repingdon, even the Mayor of Leicester suggested she write a book.

Perhaps she could have Fr. Spryngolde help write her book, her parish priest, counselor, and confessor who stood by her all these years, who knew all of her trials and temptations, who had repeatedly questioned her about her visions. So on July 23, 1436, the feast day of her beloved St. Bridget, Margery started to talk as Fr. Spryngolde wrote her words down, her faith in God and Jesus enduring. Another vision from God came to Margery, "Daughter, by this book many shall be turned to me and believe."

Ackroyd, Peter. *The Canterbury Tales, Geoffrey Chaucer: A Retelling*. New York: Viking, 2010.

Arnold, John H., and Katherine J. Lewis. *A Companion to the Book of Margery Kempe*. Rochester, N.Y.: D.S. Brewer, 2004.

Aston, Margaret. *Lollards and Reformers: Images and Literacy in Late Medieval Religion*. London: Continuum, 1984.

Atkinson, Clarissa W. *Mystic and Pilgrim: The Book and the World of Margery Kempe*. Ithaca, N.Y.: Cornell University Press, 1983.

Bartlett, Anne Clark, and Thomas Howard Bestul, eds. *Cultures of Piety: Medieval English Devotional Literature in Translation*. Ithaca, N.Y.: Cornell University Press, 1999.

Beckwith, Sarah. "A Very Material Mysticism: The Medieval Mysticism of Margery Kempe." In David Aers, ed., *Medieval Literature: Criticism, Ideology and History*. Brighton, U.K.: Harvester, 1986

———. "The Uses of Corpus Christi and The Book of Margery Kempe." In *Christ's Body: Identity, Culture and Society in Late Medieval Writings*.: London: Routledge, 1993.

Bennett, Judith M., and Charles Warren Hollister. *Medieval Europe: A Short History*. 11th Edition. New York: McGraw-Hill, 2011.

Bhattacharji, Santha. *God Is an Earthquake: The Spirituality of Margery Kempe*. London: Darton, Longman and Todd, 1997.

Blomefield, Francis. *An essay towards a topographical history of the county of Norfolk*. London: William Miller, 1805.

Boyd, Beverly. "Wyclif, Joan of Arc, and Margery Kempe," *Mystics Quarterly,* vol. 12, no. 3 (1986).

Brie, Friedrich W.D. *The Brut, or the Chronicles of England*. London: Kegan Paul, Trench, Trubner, 1906.

Chaucer, Geoffrey. *The Canterbury Tales*. New York: Penguin, 2003.

Collis, Louise. *Memoirs of a Medieval Woman: The Life and Times of Margery Kempe*. New York: Harper and Row, 1964.

Davey, Francis, ed. *The Itineraries of William Wey*. Oxford: Bodleian Library, 2010.

de Soto, Jesús Huerta. *Money, Bank Credit, and Economic Cycles*. Melinda A. Stroup, trans. Auburn, Ala.: Ludwig von Mises Institute, 2006.

de Worde, Wynken. *The Boke of Keruynge (Book of Carving)*. Peter Brears, trans. Sheffield, U.K.: Equinox, 2003.

Duffy, Eamon. *The Stripping of the Altars: Traditional Religion in England, 1400–1580*. 2nd edition. New Haven, Conn.: Yale University Press, 2005.

Forrest, Ian. *The Detection of Heresy in Late Medieval England*. Oxford: Oxford University Press, 2005.

Foxe, John. *Foxe's Book of Martyrs*. W. Grinton Berry, ed. Grand Rapids: Revell, 1998.

Fritze, Ronald, and William Baxter Robison, eds. *Historical Dictionary of Late Medieval England: 1272–1485*. Westport, Conn.: Greenwood, 2002.

Gallyon, Margaret. *Margery Kempe of Lynn and Medieval England*. Norwich, U.K.: Canterbury, 1995.

Given-Wilson, Chris, ed. *Fourteenth Century England*, vol. II. Woodbridge, Suffolk: Boydell, 2002.

Glenn, Cheryl. "Popular Literacy in the Middle Ages: *The Book of Margery Kempe*," in *Popular Literacy: Studies in Cultural Practices and Poetics*. John Trimbur, ed. Pittsburgh: University of Pittsburgh Press, 2001.

Goodman, Anthony. *Margery Kempe and Her World*. New York: Routledge, 2002.

Graves, Edgar, ed. *A Bibliography of English History to 1485: Based on the Sources and Literature of English History from the Earliest Times to about 1485 by Charles Gross*. New York: Clarendon, 1975.

Hildesley, C. Hugh. *Journeying with Julian*. New York: Morehouse, 1993.

Hillen, Henry J. *History of the Borough of King's Lynn*. Darlington, U.K.: EP, 1978.

Hirsh, John C. *The Revelations of Margery Kempe: Paramystical Practices in Late Medieval England*. Leiden: E.J. Brill, 1989.

Hudson, Anne. *The Premature Reformation: Wycliffite Texts and Lollard History*. New York: Clarendon, 2002.

John-Julian, Fr. *The Complete Julian of Norwich*. Brewster, Mass.: Paraclete, 2009.

Johnston, William, ed. *The Cloud of Unknowing and The Book of Privy Counseling*. New York: Doubleday, 1973.

Julian of Norwich. *A Lesson of Love: The Revelations of Julian of Norwich (Unabridged): Translated and Appointed for Daily Reading by Father John-Julian, O.J.N.* New York: Walker, 1998.

———. *Revelation of Love*. John Skinner, trans. New York: Bantam Doubleday Dell, 1996.

Kelly, John. *The Great Mortality: An Intimate History of the Black Death, the Most Devastating Plague of All Time*. New York: Harper Perennial, 2006.

Kempe, Margery. *The Book of Margery Kempe, 1436.* W. Butler-Bowdon, ed. R.W. Chambers, intro. London: Jonathan Cape, 1936.

———. *The Book of Margery Kempe.* Barry A. Windeatt, trans. London: Penguin, 2004.

———. *The Book of Margery Kempe.* Sanford Brown Meech, ed., with prefatory note by Hope Emily Allen. Oxford: Oxford University Press, 1940.

———. *The Book of Margery Kempe.* Lynn Staley, ed. and trans. New York: Norton, 2001.

Lacey, Robert. *Great Tales From English History: A Treasury of True Stories about the Extraordinary People—Knights, Knaves, Rebels and Heroes, Queens and Commoners—Who Made Britain Great.* New York: Little Brown, 2007.

Lochrie, Karma. *Margery Kempe and Translations of the Flesh.* Philadelphia: University of Pennsylvania Press, 1991.

———. "The Book of Margery Kempe: The Marginal Woman's Quest for Literary Authority," *Journal of Medieval and Renaissance Studies* 16, 1986.

Lowe, Ben. "Teaching in the 'Schole of Christ': Law, Learning, and Love in Early Lollard Pacifism," *Catholic Historical Review* vol. 90, no. 3, 2004.

Lutton, Robert. *Lollardy and Orthodox Religion in Pre-Reformation England.* Suffolk, U.K.: Boydell and Brewer, 2006.

McFarlane, K.B. *The Origins of Religious Dissent in England.* New York: Collier, 1952.

Mortimer, Ian. *The Fears of Henry IV: The Life of England's Self-Made King.* London: Vintage, 2008.

———. *The Time Traveler's Guide to Medieval England: A Handbook for Visitors to the Fourteenth Century.* New York: Touchstone, 2008.

Oman, Sir Charles William Chadwick. *The Great Revolt of 1381.* London: University of Oxford Press, 1906.

Owen, Dorothy M. *The Making of King's Lynn: A Documentary Survey.* London: Oxford University Press for the British Academy, 1984.

Pernoud, Regine, and Marie-Veronique Clin. *Joan of Arc: Her Story.* Jeremy duQuesnay Adams, trans. New York: St. Martin's, 1999.

Pitard, Derrick G. "A Selected Bibliography for Lollard Studies," in *Lollards and their Influence in Late Medieval England.* Fiona Somerset, et al., eds. Suffolk, U.K.: Boydell, 2003.

Rex, Richard. *The Lollards* (Social History in Perspective). New York: Palgrave, 2002.

Rolle, Richard. *The Fire of Love.* Clifton Wolters, trans. New York: Penguin, 2012.

Roman, Christopher. *Domestic Mysticism in Margery Kempe and Dame Julian of Norwich: The Transformation of Christian Spirituality in the Late Middle Ages.* Lewiston, N.Y.: Edwin Mellen, 2005.

Saul, Nigel, ed. *The Oxford Illustrated History of Medieval England.* New York: Oxford University Press, 1997.

Shakespeare, William. *Four Great Histories: Henry IV: Part I, Henry IV: Part 2, Henry V, and Richard III.* Mineola, N.Y.: Dover, 2006.

Shirley, W.W. *A Catalogue of the Original Works of John Wyclif.* Oxford, 1865.

Staley, Lynn. *Margery Kempe's Dissenting Fictions.* University Park, Penn.: Pennsylvania State University Press, 1994.

Strohm, Paul. *England's Empty Throne: Usurpation and the Language of Legitimation, 1399–1422.* Glasgow: Bell and Bain, 1998.

Swanson, R.N. "Will the Real Margery Kempe Please Stand Up!" in Diana Wood, ed., *Women and Religion in Medieval England.* Oxford, U.K.: Oxbow, 2003.

Tanner, Norman P. *Heresy Trials in the Diocese of Norwich, 1428-31.* London: The Royal Historical Society, 1977.

Watt, Diane. *Secretaries of God: Women Prophets in Late Mediaeval and Early Modern England.* Cambridge, U.K.: D.S. Brewer, 1997.

———. *Medieval Women's Writing.* Cambridge, U.K.: Polity, 2007.

Wey, Francis. *Rome.* Philadelphia: International, 1897.

Wey, William. *An English Pilgrim to Compostella in 1456.* Francis Davey, ed. and trans. London: Confraternity of Saint James, 2000.

Witalisz, Wladislaw, "Authority and the Female Voice in Middle English Mystical Writings: Julian of Norwich and Margery Kempe," in *Homo Narrans: Texts and Essays in Honor of Jerome Klinkowitz.* Zygmunt Mazur and Richard Utz, eds. Cracow: Jagiellonian University Press, 2004.